Laura Maya

TELL THEM MY NAME

Laura Maya

TELL THEM MY NAME

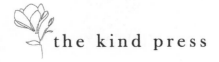

the kind press

Copyright © 2022 Laura Maya
First published by the kind press, 2022

This book is memoir. It reflects the author's present recollections of experiences over time. Some names and characteristics have been changed, some events have been compressed and some dialogue has been recreated. This publication contains the opinions and ideas of its author. It is intended to provide helpful and informative material on the subjects addressed in the publication. While the publisher and author have used their best efforts in preparing this book, the material in this book is of the nature of general comment only.

Cover design by Nada Backovic
Internal design: Nikki Jane Designs, Nicola Matthews
Editing: Emily Miller and Dr Juliet Richters
Photos: Miha Mohoric, Nina Behek, David Frot

Cataloguing-in-Publication
entry is available from the
National Library Australia.

NATIONAL
LIBRARY
OF AUSTRALIA

ISBN: 978-0-6451392-8-0
ISBN: 978-0-6451392-7-3 (ebook)

This book is dedicated to 'Oma' Dorothy, 'Opa' Bert, and my 'Swedish dad', Jan—three loved ones who encouraged me to write and insisted I had a book in me, but died before I could prove they were right.

This book is also dedicated to the farmers of the world. None of us would be here without you.

Contents

Preface

Bad language and other important things

People often tell me I'm gifted with languages and I used to believe them. Since my teens, I've been a borderline obsessive culture geek who takes steps to learn languages that others might consider extreme. Like wallpapering my entire house with Spanish verb conjugations scrawled on post-it notes. Or moving to Spain.

So, when I found myself living in a remote Himalayan village with a Nepali family who could not speak any English, I wasn't worried at first. I was confident I would learn the language easily. After all, I'd already learnt Norwegian, Spanish and French while living in Norway, Spain and France. I'd read and studied and taken classes, but I also believed in the 'learning by osmosis' theory. I thought I learnt languages quickly because I immersed myself in the culture and surrounded myself with locals, so my brain absorbed the words like some kind of mystical sponge.

The first six months learning a language are the hardest—an arduous, uphill slog memorising words I can't pronounce and stringing them together using grammar rules that make no sense. Then, when I find myself able to hold basic conversations about food and the weather, I hit a momentous peak. From there, my ability to speak the language usually accelerates at the speed of skipping merrily down the other side of the hill.

However, despite coming and going from Nepal for over five years and being completely immersed in Himalayan village culture, I've never conquered my Nepali language mountain. Maybe it's because visa restrictions prevent us from staying in Nepal for more than five months each year, so I forget my progress between visits. Or perhaps it's because despite memorising the squiggly letters of the Devanagari alphabet, I can still only sound out words like a *Sesame Street* monster.

In short, my Nepali sucks. Which is not quite the language level I was aiming for when it became the sole means of communication between me and two Nepali elders as we travelled through Europe together for a month. We were taking them from the only life they'd ever known in the Himalayas to an alien world where almost everything they saw and experienced would require extensive explanation.

Our Nepali 'parents', Aama and Baba, are indigenous Gurung people. They are native speakers of the Tibeto-Burman language Tamu Kyi, also known as Tamu or the Gurung language. My mother tongue is English and my husband David's is French. Our only common language is Nepali (or Nepalese, depending on who you ask), and once we left Nepal we would be Aama and Baba's only translators, responsible for explaining everything from politics to religion to how to use the toilet and why dinosaurs became extinct. Charades and Pictionary could only take us so far.

When I began writing this book, I realised it would be impossible to translate our conversations exactly as they happened. We had a vocabulary of several hundred Nepali words, but we struggled to string them together. We spoke like cavemen, so instead of saying 'Welcome! Please have a seat,' it sounded more like, 'You. There. Sit. Now. Ugh!' And when Aama and Baba spoke, we only caught three-quarters of the words in each sentence. Aama developed such a unique and effective sign language to accompany her speech when talking to us that a lot of comprehension came from what was unspoken.

At the same time, conversations that would take five minutes between two native speakers sometimes took days or even weeks. We had to repeat ourselves constantly, flick through dictionaries, check words in Google Translate and sometimes we even had to phone a bilingual friend in Nepal. None of which makes great reading.

So, to make this book more enjoyable for you, I've written our conversations as if they flowed without interruption. If we discussed a topic over dinner one night, in the car the next day and a week later on a train when we had finally gathered the vocabulary to understand each other, I've written it as if the entire conversation took place in just one of those locations, and without all the faffing around and frustration of finding the right words. I've also written what we were trying to say and what we understood, rather than translating the stilted, messy interactions that often took place. I should also mention there is a little swearing in these pages, but (if it's any consolation) nowhere near as much as there was in real life.

With the exception of me, my husband and my Nepali parents, I've changed the names of everyone in this book, whether they asked me to or not. Then I blended some 'characters' together to make it easier for readers to follow the wild and untamed branches of our Nepali and French family trees. I've also changed the name of Aama and Baba's remote village (not that it appears on many maps anyway) to protect the privacy of the people I love who call it home.

The final and most important thing to note is that this book is my interpretation of our story, as understood and witnessed by my own experience of the world and through the lens of my personal culture and languages. I've written this for you not as an expert on Nepali, Gurung, European or even Australian culture, but as a flawed and bumbling student. As a woman cloaked in the privilege of white skin, I've felt unsure if it's appropriate for me to tell the stories of my Gurung friends at all, even if they encouraged me to write them because they cannot. I understand that great damage can be done to people of colour when their narrative is whitewashed and exploited by those who can't understand or relate to their lived experience. There are so many gaps in my knowledge about the cultures represented in this book that doing them justice has felt nearly impossible at every stage of the process. I wrote this book because Aama, Baba, David and I all knew in our hearts this journey was something extraordinary and needed to be shared with the world. There are countless books out there about white travellers from rich countries visiting impoverished nations and having some kind of transformation, but this was a unique opportunity to flip that narrative on its head. Unfortunately, however, the only way I can tell this story is still from my own point of view.

I also spent much of this great adventure translating conversations between Nepali and French, neither of which is my mother tongue. It was inevitable things would get lost in translation, and I've been so afraid of making a mess of it that I almost gave up. But I made a promise to Aama and Baba that I would write our story, and eventually the fear of letting them down became more unbearable than the fear of getting it wrong. I've scrutinised every word in this book in an effort to accurately represent the people I love whose stories are engraved in these pages. By the time you read this, these words will have passed through the hands of many editors, including Aama and Baba's talented granddaughter and a professional Sensitivity Reader, in an attempt to uncover linguistic or cultural errors and any unconscious bias that might cloud my understanding of our journey together. But I have no doubt I have still got things wrong. I'm learning. We all are. I trust that any failures on my part will spark important conversations and teachable moments the world and I need right now.

This book was written with abundant love and all the best intentions, but there are at least twenty different versions of this unusual tale.

Today, I invite you to read just one of them.

A nod to the gods
In Nepal, reaching the age of eighty-four is an important

milestone. After this birthday, you become 'godlike' in the eyes of your family, friends and community, which is a pretty big deal. A ceremonial event called *chaurasi puja* is usually held to celebrate your longevity, during which time family and friends come together to perform rituals and offer gifts to the mortal god in exchange for a blessing.

Each family marks the occasion in different ways, but a common theme is the number eighty-four. In honour of the person's eighty-four years, eighty-four pots of water or wheat are often placed throughout the house, or eighty-four different foods or meals prepared to offer first to the gods, then later to the people who attend the ceremony. As part of the *puja*, the family also offers a cow to their priest with the belief this opens the door to heaven.

In 2020, we were due to travel to Nepal to celebrate our Baba's *chaurasi puja* in the months following his eighty-fourth birthday.

Then the coronavirus pandemic hit and the Australian borders were slammed shut, locking us inside. Aama and Baba were also locked down in their remote mountain village in Nepal, unable to even buy food or access basic healthcare, let alone throw a party fit for a god.

So, to honour our Nepali parents and their impact on my life, I have divided this book not into traditional chapters but eighty-four pots.

Eighty-four stories.

Eighty-four stepping stones that show how, when placed side by side, we can create a pathway where a bunch of total strangers without a common language, bloodline or culture can walk through the world together as family.

PART 1

Nepal

The world does not need white people to civilize others.
The real White People's Burden is to civilize ourselves.
—*Robert Jensen, The Heart of Whiteness:*
Confronting Race, Racism, and White Privilege

1

We have travelled to Nepal to make an impossible dream come true. At least it *feels* impossible to me right now—trekking through the Himalayas with all the avalanches, altitude sickness, hypothermia and a complete absence of any fitness on my part. When we reach the base camp of the highest mountain on earth I expect to feel proud of such an incredible achievement. Instead, all I feel is *relief*—that I didn't die and that my husband, David, has decided he's come far enough and strikes 'Summit Everest' from his bucket list forever.

Nepal is home to eight of the world's ten highest mountain peaks and the birthplace of Buddha. The trekking and tourism industry is booming right now, despite ongoing political unrest as the country recovers from a violent civil war. Poverty is widespread and we're told there are plenty of volunteer opportunities for travellers who want to stay on in Nepal after their trek and 'give something back'. So, when we return from Everest's Solukhumbu District to the capital city of Kathmandu, we connect with a local non-governmental organisation who, according to their website, are looking for help. They tell us they need a volunteer team to establish a new project in a village where they've never worked before. It's a four-month assignment in a remote mountain community called Sundara, which has no electricity or roads and can only be accessed on foot. All we know is that the local school has asked if someone can come and build the mountain's first children's library. We have no idea if they expect us to knock together an actual building with our soft, feeble hands, project manage the library's construction or find an existing room and fill it with books … and we're not really qualified to do any of those things. Whenever we ask the NGO staff to be more specific, they say, 'Don't worry! Everything is possible in Nepal!' Encouraged by their optimism, we put our hands up for the job and embark on the two-day journey from Kathmandu to Sundara.

The rural school where we'll be working is perched on the side of a mountain between two villages. Thousands of stone steps stretch above and below the simple whitewashed building where about 150 students gather each day to get a basic education. On one side of the school is dense jungle, and on the other is an open valley with terraced farmland carved into the earth on every hillside—like a giant's stairway to the sky. In the distance, white and terracotta mudbrick houses nestle in fields of yellow mustard flowers. Women carry baskets loaded with firewood on their backs and men drive their oxen through the fields. Beyond the village lie the snow-capped peaks of the Himalayas, with the sacred mountain Macchapuchre in the centre, rising behind the school like an enormous white fishtail. The crisp winter air is thick with the smell of smouldering kitchen fires and stale incense from this morning's prayers. It's also a bit thinner on oxygen than we're used to, so our heads feel light and our feet a little heavier as we climb the stairs to the school.

The school itself is a simple stone building with six dark and damp classrooms, each with a few rows of wooden desks and benches, all splintered and decayed. The only thing on the wall is the blackboard. There is no colour in the rooms, no books, no lights, no posters, no visible signs of life. Other than the children. When we arrive, we're officially welcomed to the school in a grand ceremony. All the children and teachers gather outside and we sit at a table of honour. The students place garlands of yellow, orange and purple flowers around our necks and we sit in the sun for hours, our skin turning from white to pink to red while the teachers (almost all of whom are male) make long and impassioned speeches we cannot understand yet.

While they speak, I watch the students watching us. They're all wearing the same uniform: blue skirts or pants on the bottom, white shirts on top and bright red bows in the girls' plaited hair. I can't help but think how strange we must look to them. David with his messy 'beginner' dreadlocks, me in harem pants and a hemp top in various shades of 'earthy' green. My outfit looks a bit like the Nepali women's traditional *salwar kameez* but nowhere near as beautiful or vibrant. Or clean. Or ironed. I'm also wearing a scarf on my head like a dodgy fortune teller, purple crepe with thin strips of tinsel threaded through it. To us, we just look like the countless other Westerners who reject the status quo and run off to mystical Nepal to 'find themselves'. But I imagine the students sitting in front of us are wondering, 'What could these people possibly do to help or teach us if they don't even know how to comb their hair?'

There is only one presentable and respectable member of our group helping us raise the bar: my beautiful mother-in-law, Véronique. A doting mum, she promised David she would fly to meet him wherever he was in the world on his thirtieth birthday, a promise she made knowing her son loves tropical islands and turquoise ocean and her chances of spending a month in Tahiti were pretty good. Véronique is an accountant for a huge corporate enterprise in Paris. She's strong, demure and, like most French women, always immaculately put together. But for a few weeks every year she trades her heels for hiking boots, escapes the traffic and pollution of Paris and joins her globetrotting son for an adventure somewhere in the world. This is the first time, however, he has led her so far off the beaten path. Not only will we be working in a remote Himalayan village with no internet, electricity or reflective surfaces, but for the next four months we'll be living in a house made of mud with a family of indigenous farmers we have no way to communicate with.

2

Our host, Dar Kumari Gurung, is shorter and older than all of us, but she exudes strength and an almost regal presence. Her traditional *lungi* skirt is forest green, adorned with leaves and spirals, and she wears a red velvet long-sleeved *cholo* vest, crossed and tied across her chest. There is a tiny gold stud on the left side of Dar Kumari's nose and more than twenty thick gold hoops of various sizes cling to her drooping earlobes.

Somehow she manages to smile with every part of her face.

When we meet for the first time, Dar Kumari clasps her palms together and the glass bangles around her wrists jingle like tiny bells.

'*Namaste!*' her eyes twinkle as she busies herself; pulling out stools made from old tyres and laying a handwoven straw mat on the mud-packed verandah where she wants us to sit down. We're three desperately unfit foreigners who have just staggered up her mountain in the blistering midday sun and we arrive looking like we've crawled here through the desert in search of water. Dar Kumari grips my sunburnt arm with exceptional force and guides me gently off my feet, prattling away in Nepali. We can't understand a word she's saying but somehow it's clear she has never seen this shade of red on a human face before and she's concerned our heads might implode.

As she runs around, fetching water and boiling it on the fire, I take in my surroundings. We're sitting in the stone courtyard of a two-storey mudbrick house. It's painted red terracotta on the bottom and has been left as its natural clay brown in the middle; the tiny, uneven bricks on the top have been whitewashed. Dark wooden shutters are propped open to reveal windows covered in steel bars. Buddhist prayer flags are strung around the house so small squares of blue, white, red, green and yellow fabric flutter against a flawless cornflower sky.

Dar Kumari returns with silver cups of water and watches us as we take our first thirsty sips. She is soon joined by her son, Dhaney, who greets us with a timid smile.

'Aama,' the woman says to us, placing both hands on her

chest.

'She says you must call her Aama,' Dhaney stammers in shy, broken English. 'It means mother.'

'But she's too young to be my mother!' laughs Véronique.

In Nepal, it's customary to call people not by their given names but by their relationship to you. Even if you're not blood-related, even if it's the server waiting on your table at a restaurant, you address everyone as family. So you would call a female either mother, sister, aunt, daughter or niece, depending on her age and connection to you.

Véronique is fifty-five years old and Aama is about fifty-eight. They could be sisters, they agree, and so their place in each other's lives is established. Dar Kumari is the older sister, *didi,* and Véronique is the younger sister, *bahini.* Because in Nepal the child of your sibling is considered a child of your own, Dar Kumari adopts David to be her son, *chora.* And that automatically makes me her daughter-in-law.

With my limited understanding of Nepali village culture so far, it seems to me a daughter-in-law's role is to tirelessly perform household chores, produce children, work in the fields, cook, clean and wash everyone's dirty clothes. This isn't great news for me, because they're all things I've either made a conscious decision not to do or happen to really suck at.

It's okay, though, because I'll soon discover in Nepal I suck at *everything.* In our first months in the village, we have to unlearn all the things we think we know about how to survive in the world. Even the most routine and mundane tasks are performed differently here, so we need to relearn how to eat, crap, sleep and speak—ideally without transgressing all the social norms that don't feel normal to us yet. At mealtimes, our hosts use their right hands to scoop their traditional meal of *dhal bhat* (lentils and rice) from their plates to their mouths—*never* the left hand, that's reserved for wiping your bum. Whenever I try to eat with my hand, I come away looking as though I've been in a food fight, with grains of rice lodged in all the wrong face holes. We're like toddlers again in every way, struggling to communicate in one-word sentences. Rice. Delicious ... Me. Sleep ... That. Difficult ...

Hygiene is also an issue. Instead of toilet paper there's just a bucket of water next to the toilet, but I can't figure out how to wash my nether regions without spending the rest of the day pulling my soggy knickers out of my crack. The porcelain squat toilet tapers at one end and has a hole at the other. I have no idea if you're supposed to squat over the hole and pee towards the skinny end of the bowl, or squat at the skinny end and *aim* for the hole. I just focus on precision and hope for the best. There's also no shower in the village so everyone cleans themselves in the very public communal water source in Aama's courtyard. The local women wash with the underskirts of their traditional *lungi* pulled up to their armpits, but unfortunately, on this great adventure I forgot to pack my petticoat. So, I try to wash by lathering up my skin *and* clothes at the same time while the villagers watch, howling with laughter. Eventually I stop showering altogether.

As a fully grown adult human, I'm shocked to suddenly find myself incapable of performing life's most basic tasks. Given we're no longer able to feed or wash ourselves with confidence, it should occur to us that we're not exactly qualified to build a children's library in a country and culture we know nothing about, with little more than thirty words for communication.

But off we go …

In the first few weeks we work with some local carpenters to transform a crumbling, dark, old storeroom into the Sunflower Children's Resource Centre, a rainbow library and study space with white walls, emerald green shutters, sapphire blue carpet and red and yellow chairs and tables. One sunny, winter afternoon, over a hundred people gather at the school to witness a red ribbon being placed across the door then sliced with great ceremony and a rusty pair of scissors. The first library on the mountain is officially open and the kids go *berserk*. They run around the room, climbing the furniture and screaming with delight at everything they touch. They've never seen picture books before and they seize them with such intensity that the pages rip and crumple in their grip. They fight over everything, snatching and wrestling pencils and puzzles from each other's hands while David, Véronique and I flap around like hysterical pigeons, squawking at them to calm down. Half an hour after the doors open, a not insignificant number of books and games are already destroyed.

This is the first time it occurs to us that we have absolutely no idea what we're doing.

3

It's not unusual for me to be so unprepared. I've never been much of a planner, really. All my life I've been restless. Insatiably curious. Always jumping from one thing to the next in search of … kind of *everything*.

I left my home in Australia in 2001 when I was twenty-one years old and I've been wandering the world ever since, just following my odd-shaped nose. I worked as a nanny in Spain for a while, a tax auditor in the Netherlands, a barbecue chef in Italy and even became a certified sailor while managing a bar on a luxury cruise ship in Scotland. At some point in my travels, it dawned on me that I enjoyed certain unearned privileges denied to many others, both overseas and in my own country. My parents were determined to give me the kind of opportunities they only dreamed of growing up. I watched them work themselves to exhaustion to give me and my sister financial stability, a comfortable life and a launching pad to chase all our wildest dreams. But I already had a distinct advantage as a white, educated, able-bodied (albeit female) Australian who was born on a conflict-free and economically secure patch of dirt with free healthcare. When I was suddenly struck by my own good fortune I, like a lot of idealistic twenty-somethings, decided the best way to reconcile this great global imbalance was to volunteer abroad. Although I possessed staggeringly few useful or tangible skills, I believed I could 'make a difference' somehow. So off I went. I volunteered as a journalist in

Honduras and helped build a mudbrick house for a young Lencan family who had lost their home in a hurricane. I also spent some time in the Amazon rainforest in Ecuador, working with a group of indigenous people on a tourism project. Along the way, I met children who lived with vultures among the mounds of rubbish at a city tip, eating rotten, slimy food scraps from steaming piles of garbage. I interviewed murderers and rapists from notorious gangs while living in a city with some of the highest homicide rates in the world. And I encountered teenage girls married to octogenarians in the jungle—children giving birth to the children of ageing shamans in order to keep the community's mystical bloodlines strong.

The world never quite looked the same to me after that.

Despite my best intentions, I don't think I did a single thing to create a lasting, positive change for the people I set out to help. However, these experiences changed *me* forever, and since then I've never quite found my way back to the beaten path. It's like there's always a chasm between me and where I think modern society expects me to be. When I look around at my friends and family, most people appear capable and confident moving through the phases of life generally mapped out for us: from school, to work, to marriage, to home ownership, to children and eventually, a schmick luxury caravan in which to spend a well-earned retirement travelling around Australia. The people in my life all seem to have beautiful homes with well-kept gardens and a sturdy back deck where they can relax after work with a glass of wine. They're busy building on their already successful careers and earning larger salaries every year. They can soothe their wanderlust with an annual overseas holiday and, for the most part, everyone seems to know how to cook.

But not me. I'm pushing thirty and I'm struggling to hit any of these obvious markers of adulthood.

I can hitch a ride from the Pacific Ocean to the Caribbean Sea in the back of several strangers' pick-up trucks without getting killed, but don't ask me to keep a basil plant alive for a week. I can also coordinate flights on twelve different budget airlines to circumnavigate the entire world for less than a thousand dollars, but if you start talking about bathroom renovations and home loan interest rates, you have lost me.

For me, navigating these 'normal' things feels a bit like trying to give a llama a piggyback. Awkward. Difficult. Maybe even impossible.

The only remotely grown-up thing I did in my twenties was to get married. The first time I met my husband, David, he was perched on a stool in the lobby bar of the hotel where I was staying in Peru. He had bronze skin, dusty sun-kissed hair and an accent that made every word sound like a late-night love song dedication. When it came to romantic relationships, the odds were stacked against me. How would I ever find another nomadic soul who was content to wander the world aimlessly, as I was? So, meeting David was a bit like winning the lottery then immediately getting struck by lightning. He was a Frenchman who had been working and travelling his way around the world for three years longer than me, with no end goal and no idea where he was headed next. He was my perfect match. David and I fell in love within seconds of meeting each other, which was uncomfortable and unfortunate because his new girlfriend of three days was sitting next to him at the time. Nothing happened between us in South America, but we stayed in touch after going our separate ways. When we both found ourselves single and living in Australia about three years later, we decided—without much thought or fanfare—to bind ourselves together for life.

Eighteen months after our impromptu wedding we moved back to France, where my goal was to learn French and have my first conversation with David's parents. I'd always dreamed of moving to Paris some day and cycling to work on a cobblestoned street past the Eiffel Tower while wearing a red beret and a stylish winter coat. But for the most part, life in France was not quite the romantic scene from *Amélie* I'd pictured in my head. We lived in a ten-square-metre apartment in a tiny village in the French Alps; our bunk beds wedged between the toilet and the fridge. I was working six days a week in a shop selling technical sportswear in a language I couldn't speak, and my commute to work was a sweaty uphill trudge through the snow wearing a ski suit. I could tell that David and I were emerging from the honeymoon phase of our marriage because I'd stopped trying to hold my farts in when he was around. We were still in love, but we were starting to pull back from each other just enough to look out at the world around us again. Until then we'd been completely focused on our marriage—two strangers working out how to be a husband and wife who had no home base, spoke different languages and came from different cultures.

Neither of us were ever keen on the idea of having children, but once we were married, people kept clucking and making high-pitched sing-song remarks about the shelf life of my ovaries.

At the age of twenty-nine, we were both teetering on the edge of a full-blown life crisis. David was furious at himself because he still hadn't got around to climbing Mount Everest. Meanwhile, I was feeling guilty that my dead-end retail job was, I suspected, the last link in a questionable global supply chain that exploits Bangladeshi garment workers. Shouldn't I be doing more for the world?

4

The rhythm of village life is like a catchy song. Once I hear it a few times, I find myself singing along even if I don't know the words. Despite our unfamiliar surroundings, or perhaps because of them, we soon fall into the solace of routine. We seek comfort in the sameness we find from one day to the next so the things that feel foreign slowly become familiar.

Every morning with the first light, we wake to the drumroll of water falling from the courtyard tap into an empty plastic bucket. Aama and her daughter-in-law murmur in hushed tones and prepare their morning *puja*, the Buddhist ceremonial prayers that take place each day at dawn and dusk. Two tiny bells kiss gently and their chime rings in the air alongside the musty smell of incense. Then for a few moments there is complete silence in the valley.

The peace of morning *puja* is broken by a heavy tin can clanging on the floor of the buffalo stable next to the toilet, followed by the steady beat of milk squirting onto metal. Aama is squatting beneath the buffalo, the soles of her cracked, bare feet sitting flat on the concrete floor. The layers of her *lungi* skirt, now gathered in her lap, are held in place by a thick band of bright blue material wrapped several times around her waist. A black and red floral headscarf is pulled tight over her hairline and tucked at the back to keep the wispy, greying hairs from her eyes while she works.

Each day, Aama places the milk over the fire to prepare it for our first cup of *chiya*, Nepali spiced tea, and every morning we tell her not to worry because we're running late to open the library for the kids at seven. Then, she waves her hands around furiously, telling us to sit down and wait because this is Nepal and no one goes anywhere or does anything in the morning until they've had their bloody tea (I'm paraphrasing). She also insists on feeding us breakfast so we won't get hungry before *second* breakfast is served at ten.

We arrive at the library every morning just as the sun peeks over the Himalayas and floods the room with amber light. About five children are waiting for the doors to open but by the time we close at nine, there are up to fifty students crammed inside, often yelling, hitting and biting each other. We've built a community library, but in the beginning, the children have no interest in reading at all. Until now, their only experience of paper that is bound and covered with words has been textbooks—the contents of which they are forced by their teachers to chant and learn by rote. They don't know that books can bring them joy, that written stories can make them laugh or cry. They don't know that reading can transport them to another world. Yet. But still, they turn up at the library every day, to play and draw and hang out with the funny-looking foreigners.

One day, we introduce enforced reading time so if they want to use the toys or art supplies, they have to spend twenty minutes at least *pretending* to read a book first. After a few weeks, some of the students get hooked on reading. They huddle in the corner with their noses in their books, murmuring the words out loud because they've never learnt to read silently in their heads. One boy drops in every day on his way to cut grass for his family's buffalo. With a machete in one hand and a book in the other, he stands by the door and reads. After fifteen minutes, he hides the book between the pages of a drab-looking science encyclopedia so the other kids won't find it and he heads out to the fields. On his way back, he stops in again, now covered head to foot in mulched grass, and escapes into a few more pages before heading back home.

Most of the kids are curious enough about the library to visit at least once or twice a week, but there is one child in the school who refuses to set foot inside.

Anisha.

She's about seven years old and she makes herself known to us from day one. While other children approach us with cautious excitement, Anisha stalks up to me in the playground, her face twisted into a scowl, and thrusts her upturned palm in my face. She pinches my underarm to get my attention then stabs at her empty palm with her index finger, silently demanding I put something in it. Food. Money. Anything. Her uniform, a threadbare hand-me-down three sizes too large, hangs limp from her bony frame. I can tell by the hardened look in her eyes that she's always hungry.

I've never seen Anisha smile.

Even without speaking the language we can see she's aggressive towards the other students. Her small group of friends seem wary of her. Many of them frequent the library but Anisha refuses to join them. Instead, she stands outside an open window with her arms tucked across her chest, her chin downcast, watching her friends play without her.

'Come join us,' I stammer in Nepali whenever I see her standing alone at the window, but she only glares at me in response. Her eyes are ravenous, so when no one is looking I slip an occasional packet of biscuits into her school bag. It feels inadequate, but I know we can't feed her screaming belly without also offering to feed the entire school.

Finally, one day, Anisha takes her first hesitant step through the library doors and lingers at the entrance for an hour, watching. A few days later, she takes a seat on a bench about half a metre inside. Over the next week, Anisha inches closer to the action every day until her curiosity wins. She picks up a wooden farmyard animal puzzle and slowly inspects the colourful pieces.

No matter what rules we have in place, Anisha *refuses* to read, as if touching the books might burn and scar her fingers.

She's far more comfortable playing with the toys but she's not great at sharing and often snatches objects and thumps other children over the head with them to get what she wants.

That's not unusual, though, because violent outbursts are common in the library. The kids are fun and energetic, but there are times when they become aggressive and lash out at each other, for no obvious reason at all. My guess is that they're tired because many of them walk an hour up and down the hill to get to and from school every day. It will be another couple of months before I realise this naive guess is wrong.

5

We share Aama's home with three other people. There is Aama's husband, Nar Bahadur Gurung, who we call Baba (father). There is also their youngest son, Dhaney (who is still unmarried) and their daughter-in-law, Kashi, whose husband (their eldest son) is working on a building site in the Middle East. There is also a teenage boy named Rakesh who lives *around* the house. Not inside. But that's a complicated story so I'll come back to it.

In our brief pre-project orientation by the NGO, we were told that it's rare for women in rural Nepal to hold positions of power, but it appears my new Nepali mother-in-law never got the memo. Aama's house feels like the village headquarters, with people dropping in at all hours of the day and night to have animated and important-sounding conversations we cannot decipher. When women want to know if their babies are developing well, they bring them to Aama's house. The scales donated to the village by the United Nations to measure their infants' weight hang on Aama's verandah, and the health of every child on the mountain is tracked in a notebook that she keeps in her bedroom drawer. When the community wants to slaughter a buffalo, Aama's courtyard becomes a butcher's block, the hub where meat and gizzards are distributed to every family in the village. It seems that every couple of days, Aama ducks off for meetings with the *Aama Samuha* (mothers' group), the health clinic development committee, the village development committee and the school development committee. Even though I'm not sure if Aama ever went to school herself or even knows how to read or write.

In addition to running the mountain, Aama manages her household and farmland alongside Baba, Kashi and Dhaney. Dotted all over the mountain, they have several terraced fields of rice, mustard, corn and millet seeds. The latter of these grains is used to make the local alcohol, *raksi*. They also have a well-tended vegetable garden with cauliflower, spinach, beans, potatoes, chilli, turmeric and some other seasonal vegetables, herbs and spices. In the summer months, when many crops don't grow, they forage for 'jungle vegetables' in the surrounding forest. There are also several traditional log beehives situated around the house, which Aama smokes out to harvest honey now and then. Aside from the lentils in our soup and the black tea in our *chiya*, everything that goes into our bodies here is pulled from the ground within 300 metres of where we sleep.

When it comes to food, there is a sacred code of hospitality in Nepal, and Aama takes it to an extreme. Most Nepali people eat two large meals each day, one at around ten in the morning and the other at seven in the evening, as well as a decent-sized snack at three in the afternoon. However, Aama prepares four meals for us each day, *plus* snacks. From now on, our bodyweight is a billboard that shows everyone on the mountain how well Aama is taking care of us, and she is determined to fatten us up.

The United Nations ranks countries based on their body fat ratio and currently, Nepal is the second thinnest nation on earth. Many Nepali people are so poor they're starving, so a healthy, nourished body may be considered a sign of comparable wealth. Right now, after a month of high altitude trekking in the Himalayas and a severe bout of pizza-induced dysentery in Kathmandu, I'm looking about as healthy as my vagabond bank balance. So, at mealtimes, Aama dishes me up an enormous mountain of rice fit for a yeti and the sheer sight of it makes me lose my appetite. Every meal I beg her to take half of it off my plate before I start eating and, every time, Aama grimaces like she's felt a sharp, stabbing pain in her soul. Then she transfers four grains of rice off my plate onto someone else's and looks up at me with a cheeky grin. I laugh but then, once again, plead for a smaller serving and she shakes her head and clutches her chest. Heartbroken. She then waves a single finger in the air, a symbol of my emaciated body, and makes a strangled high-pitched sound, as if the starving, sickly finger is wailing in agony. We dance this cha-cha every time we eat.

Food is just one of the many ways I feel like a disappointment to Dar Kumari Gurung. The day we met, Aama immediately accepted David as her fifth son and has adored and doted on him ever since. Every time he offers to do the washing up or help peel the potatoes, Aama's face glows with wonder and delight. What is this magnificent species of man who is willing to do women's work? Conversely, his wife, who Aama did not have the luxury of choosing as she had with her other sons, must seem grossly substandard. This daughter-in-law doesn't know how to wash her own clothes or cook *dhal bhat* and she shells beans like her hands are all thumbs. The most terrible thing of all, however, is that Aama's newly adopted French wonder god is thirty years old, married for two years and his wife hasn't produced any children for him. Even with my limited language skills, Aama has made it clear that this is a problem that needs to be solved.

6

While my apparent androgyny is a constant source of bafflement for Aama, my Nepali father-in-law, Baba, is neither concerned nor interested. Or if he is, he isn't expressing it yet in a way I can understand. He's seventy-three years old, deaf in one ear, hard of hearing in the other, and his speech is badly affected as a result. We try to communicate, but he can't decipher our

Tarzan-style Nepali and we can't make out the words he strains to speak with his gravelly voice. Not that we're accustomed to hearing it often, because Baba doesn't speak a word during the day. To anyone.

To us, Baba is an enigma. Thin and frail, his tailored buttoned-up shirt droops from his slender frame. It hangs over suit pants that are several sizes too big and which are strapped to him with a belt that could almost loop his waist twice. On his tiny head, like all Nepali men of his age, he wears a prism of colourful fabric called a *topi*. It's surprisingly formal attire for a farmer who slogs his guts out in the fields every day and climbs trees like an acrobat. It's not unusual to find him way up in the branches, looking down at us from a dizzying height while slinging a machete, slicing away foliage to feed to the buffalo. Although he says nothing, his face speaks for him when he's up there in the leaves. With an enormous, toothless grin and a wheezy chuckle, Baba seems more at home in the trees than he does with us on the ground.

When night falls, however, Baba comes alive. After sunset, when most of the family gather around the fire pit in the kitchen floor for the evening meal, Baba sits at the back of the room at a blue wooden table. Alone. Aama heats a small saucepan of *raksi*—home-brewed alcohol—and serves it warm to Baba in a chipped glass tumbler. *Raksi* in hand, Baba grins, clears his throat and speaks his first words of the day. We can't understand him, and he can't hear himself speak, but after a few sips the words rush from his mouth like a Himalayan river in the spring. He chuckles and chatters away, regardless of whether anyone is listening. From our position on the floor, we often turn and look to the back of the room and try to engage with his monologue. We laugh when he laughs but we're never sure why. After finishing his dinner, Baba slinks out of the kitchen and into the bedroom the whole family shares. He sits on the edge of his bed and cranks the pump on his battery-free radio. Then, with the volume turned up to max, he places the radio next to his good ear, lies back and strains to hear the evening news.

We are locked out of each other's worlds, yet still, Baba is not the most puzzling person we live with in Nepal. That award goes to Rakesh, the fifteen-year-old boy who sleeps in the family's buffalo stable and is not allowed to enter the house. While the rest of the family gather in the kitchen to eat and socialise in the same room, Rakesh sits outside. He has a warm face, a shy smile and a dark mop of thick wavy hair that falls in front of his often-downcast eyes. Rakesh doesn't speak much, so it's hard to get to know him. All we know is that his father died and his mother was kind of … missing. He lost contact with her after she accepted a job in the Middle East so for now, Rakesh is an orphan.

Aama and Baba seem to genuinely care about Rakesh, and they've agreed to look after him, but for some reason he's forbidden from entering their home. He sleeps in the room above the buffaloes at night and the family try to encourage him to attend school during the day. He helps in the fields when they need an extra pair of hands, and at mealtimes he waits patiently outside with the dog in the freezing Himalayan winter while everyone else eats by the fire. It's customary in Nepal that the mother of the house cooks and serves her family first before she eats. When Aama can see everyone is full and satisfied, she serves a plate for herself, Rakesh and the dog, dividing up the food left between them into equal portions. She serves Rakesh onto a plate that doesn't look like the others, which he washes up himself and keeps away from everyone else in his own room. I'm as perplexed by all of this as Aama is about my clumsy kitchen skills and barren womb. Why on earth would a child be forced to eat outside in the cold while the rest of the family gather together around a warm, cosy fire?

7

So many of the questions we were too naive to ask are answered the day we decide to start allowing students to borrow library books overnight. To prepare for this, we ask them all to make a library ID card with their name, village, parents' names and class number. This is when we discover that every child in the village has one of just three surnames: Gurung, Paudel or Nepali.

As we put names to faces, we realise the students naturally divide themselves into groups according to their surnames. When we're coordinating group games, the kids named Gurung or Paudel refuse to be on the same team as the children named Nepali. When we force them to play together, a fight always breaks out over something ridiculous. It seems that the Paudels and Gurungs are the 'cool kids' and the students named Nepali are outcasts, somehow.

While making these library cards I discover Rakesh's last name is Nepali.

So is Anisha's.

The lights go on and I can finally see what's been hidden in front of me the whole time. Hovering in the shadows is the illegal caste system, a 2000-year-old Hindu custom that divides the population into groups according to ethnicity and ranks them on a social ladder. The privileged Brahmins sit at the top and the 'impure' Dalits languish at the bottom. In Sundara, anyone whose last name is Nepali is considered a Dalit. This word means 'oppressed', and these people are literally treated as untouchable. They cannot touch people from higher castes, enter their homes or even use the same taps for water. They're forbidden to serve or touch food prepared for higher castes and they're not even allowed to eat from the same plates. This ancient custom was criminalised in 1962 in Nepal so, on paper, it doesn't exist. But 2000-year-old practices don't change overnight, and these deep-rooted beliefs still hold sway in rural Nepal.

With this deeper insight, we now understand that within the context of her own culture, the way Aama takes care of Rakesh is not cruel or harmful, but incredibly generous. She is looking after a child who society dictates her family should have no contact with and, at the same time, setting a progressive example for her community.

So, we follow Aama's lead.

In our final weeks in the village, we make it our goal to ensure the kids know the library is a safe place where everyone is equal. This is only possible because Nepali people use the English expression 'same same' in their own language. We stop letting them pick their own teams, we force the students to play with the kids they fight with the most, and when they protest in anger, we protest back.

'No!' We bark in our most authoritarian, caveman Nepali. 'You. You. Together. Play. Good. In library everyone same same!'

I could write a book the size of *War and Peace* just about the mistakes we made while setting up this library. Our greatest oversights were believing we had solutions before we truly understood the problems and failing to involve the community in every step of the development process. We just followed the NGO's vague instructions, plonked a library down in their school and expected everyone to love it. If we had consulted the community beforehand about how *they* wanted us to help, they told us later they would have much rathered we install a communal rice milk-making machine than build a library. Because on most days, a full, nourished belly is far more practical than five shelves full of books no one asked for.

We only understand as we prepare to leave the village that, despite our best intentions, we are just another pair of 'white saviours'—Western people who arrive in impoverished nations wanting to 'make a difference' but get more out of the experience for ourselves than we're able to give the people we wanted to help. We didn't take enough time to understand the people, culture and challenges the community faced before galloping in on our metaphorical white horse to try and save the day. In doing so, we contributed to Nepal's over-reliance on international aid and unwittingly became part of a system that often creates more problems for vulnerable people than it solves.

Although we came to the community to teach, in the end we were their students; another burden to take care of and an extra mouth to feed. We were aliens who didn't know how to navigate their world. With our dreadlocks and backpacker threads we were dressed like moths on a mountain full of butterflies. Yet for reasons I'll never understand, they welcomed us into their lives and embraced our crazy, pointless rainbow room full of books.

8

There is one moment in our four months in the village when I can see a tangible difference the library has made to someone's life.

It's our last week in Sundara and the children are drawing pictures. Most of the students create colourful artwork depicting their homes and fields and the mountains around us, but Anisha loves drawing flowers.

Today, she's working on an intricate rhododendron, Nepal's national flower, and colouring it with every shade of red available in the library's pencil box. When she's finished, she looks up at me and seems to hesitate. Then she rises from the floor and walks across the room to show me her masterpiece. In the past, she's shoved her drawings in her bag or tossed them in the bin, but this is the first time she's approached me to share her work.

'That's beautiful, Anisha!' I gush, with way too much enthusiasm. 'I like the different shades of red you used.'

And that's when it happens.

Her tiny cheeks tense up. Her eyes sparkle just a little and her lips curl up to meet them.

It's the first time I see Anisha smile.

'Why don't you take that home for your mum?' I ask with a big grin.

'No. You.' Anisha frowns, and as fast as the smile appears, it is gone. She presses the flower into my hands so the paper crumples and she runs for the door.

It was brief, but that moment feels like the single greatest sign of progress we've made during our time in Sundara. I didn't save Anisha from hunger or poverty, or change the trajectory of her life. But for one fleeting moment she got to experience what it felt like to be proud of herself.

The image of her smile is so powerful that it's burnt into my soul's memory forever. Which is why I will recognise it immediately when, almost three years later, I see it again.

Only this time it's not in a rural mountain village in mystical Nepal. It's 900 km away in a refuge for child sex trafficking survivors who have been rescued from an Indian brothel.

9

One often meets his destiny on the road he
takes to avoid it.
—*Grand Master Oogway in Kung Fu Panda*

Our time in Sundara has been a hilarious, frustrating,
confronting, heartwarming and enlightening experience, but
I'm ready to move on. Leaving is much harder for David, who
has achieved a sort of godlike status in the village and developed
a stronger connection with Aama and the family than I feel I
have. There is an indisputable mutual care and respect between
Aama and me, but we're women from different worlds who may
never be capable of truly understanding each other. Not that we
haven't given it a good crack. There were rare moments when
we broke through the barriers of language and culture, looked
into each other's eyes and thought, *Yes. I see you. I see beyond
our differences to the light in your soul that makes us the same.* I
am grateful to the family for welcoming us into their lives and
patiently teaching me how to live in a country and culture that
was completely foreign to me just a few months ago. But for the
most part, the village feels like a place incompatible with my
version of womanhood and I'm happy to turn the page.

The first time we see rain fall on the village is the day we
leave. We cry, the family cries and the sky weeps all over us as
we make our final trek down the mountain.

'We'll be back in two years,' I tell Aama, looking into her

eyes. We lock arms and prepare to part ways at the top of the stairs where the village meets the jungle. 'I promise.'

And at the time, I mean it. I do. But we're down to our final savings and quickly get sucked back into our 'real world'. We live in France for a year, then move back to Australia. David shaves off his dreadlocks and I retire my impressive collection of hippie headscarves. We find new jobs, I enrol in university and two years evaporate. Somewhere in that time, I pick up a book called *Not for Sale* by David Batstone and it tilts my world off its axis. In its pages, I discover that everything I'd been taught about slavery in school was a lie. Slavery was never actually abolished, it was only criminalised and forced underground, where it has developed into a $32 billion industry. In this millennium, slavery is also called 'human trafficking', and I'm shocked to discover there are more humans enslaved today than at any other time in history. Right now—today— there are children forced to become soldiers and slaughter their own families in conflict zones. Bonded labourers are dying on construction sites in the Middle East. And girls are being raped and held captive in European brothels. Once I know this is happening, I can't look away. With an all-consuming passion, I become an outspoken advocate and fundraiser for the modern abolition movement. I now know slavery is a serious issue in Nepal but as far as I can remember, I saw no signs of it in Sundara. The challenges faced by the community seem small compared to the stories I'm now hearing from trafficking victims who are abused, tortured and exploited for criminal profit. I feel guilty that I've broken my promise to Aama but I feel no great need to return to the village.

Until the day when I do.

It's been almost three years since we left Nepal and now I'm not far away, in Kolkata, India. I'm visiting a friend who is doing her thesis on global human trafficking policy and, as part of her research, we travel to the outskirts of the city to visit a refuge for teenage trafficking survivors. Over several cups of tea, the house mother talks us through the challenges the girls face from the day they are rescued from sex slavery in a brothel raid until they leave the refuge when they turn eighteen. Rehabilitation is a long, painful process and to help them reintegrate into society, all the girls are encouraged to return to school and focus on their education.

As we move to leave, we approach a flight of concrete stairs where two girls are standing in the shadows of an open doorway. They tuck their chins into their shoulders and avert their eyes as the house mother stops to introduce us.

'These girls were rescued in India but they cannot speak Hindi very well, so they require extra tuition to keep up with their studies. They are from Nepal.'

Nepal.

The word rings in my head like a gong resounding across an endless valley.

'They were trafficked here all the way from Nepal?' I gasp.

'Oh *yes*,' the house mother affirms with a wobble of her head, her tone serious. '*So* many Nepali girls are trafficked from *all* over Nepal. Nepali girls are very popular with the men here in India.'

I nod my head but my brain struggles to compute. I look back at the young girls and force a smile. One ducks back into the classroom but the other girl takes a nervous step sideways, and as she moves out of the shadow I see her face clearly for the first time.

Oh my God, she looks like Anisha.

'*Namaste,*' I croak. My brain flicks onto autopilot and I place my palms together to greet her. '*Sanchai hunuhuncha?*'

As I butcher her language with my dreadful Australian accent, the shy Nepali girl's cheeks tense into a tiny smile—the same smile that was engraved into my memory on a mountain in the Himalayas all those years ago. It's exactly as I remember it and I feel my heart stop for an eternity before the house mother introduces me to Mukti—a young girl from a remote Nepali village who is not Anisha but bears an uncanny likeness to her.

Our group continue down the concrete staircase but my feet are anchored to the floor. I can't tear my eyes away from the girl who looks like the hungry child who loved farmyard puzzles and colouring rhododendrons. If Mukti ended up trafficked into an Indian brothel and raped every day, could the same thing happen to Anisha? Could all the girls in the village be at risk of being bought and sold across the Indian border?

I return to Australia but over the following months, my mind always seems to find its way back to Mukti and Anisha. The memory of their identical smiles gnaws at me and opens a wound that won't heal until eventually, David and I decide to return to the village. We need to make sure human trafficking is at least on their radar. So, we quit our jobs, sell everything we own again, buy two plane tickets and make the long journey back to Sundara.

When we finally arrive in the village we used to call home, we're shocked by how much has changed.

Once bursting with colour and life, we find many of the village houses empty and boarded up. All over the mountain, rice terraces are abandoned and overgrown with weeds. Now there are so few students enrolled at the school that the teachers tell us it's at risk of being closed down.

Half the people in the village are gone.

10

Aama rolls out the woven mat on her mud-packed kitchen floor and gestures for us to join her by the fire. She places a glass of warm *raksi* into David's hand and a plate piled high with rice into mine.

'You look sick,' she grumbles, and I beg her to put half the rice back in the pot.

It's like no time has passed at all.

Some impressive developments have taken place since we last lived in Sundara. For a start, a terrifying yet semi-functional dirt road has been carved into the side of the mountain with a bulldozer the community pooled their resources to pay for themselves. For the first time in history, the villagers can now take a bus from the city right to their door—but only during the winter months. In the summer when the monsoon rains fall, the road moonlights as a river.

Electricity was also installed about two months ago—the shiny white light switches now a modern adornment on the houses' traditional mudbrick walls. The government allocates electricity on a schedule known as 'load shedding', so Sundara gets six hours of power each day, mostly at night when everyone's too asleep to use it. It's not a reliable connection, but it's nice to be able to charge our phones and get an occasional message out when the wind blows the 2G mobile network our way.

Another notable change is that Rakesh doesn't sit outside with the dog anymore. He's moved to another house in the village, but still comes back to help the family with their farm work and they cook him an occasional meal. Now he's allowed to sit on their doorstep with his feet *inside* the kitchen so he can join in with the family's conversations. It's literally one small step for Rakesh, but a giant leap for interethnic harmony in Nepal. I get a bit emotional when I see he's also eating off one of the family's traditional copper plates.

And the dog?

'Eaten by a tiger,' Aama says, waving a bored hand in the air and walking away.

A what?!

No one has *ever* mentioned tigers in the village before and I make a mental note to circle back to that.

The most obvious change in the village, however, is that it's remarkably devoid of life. It used to take us almost an hour to make the ten-minute journey on foot to the school because we stopped every few metres to chat with the family in each house we passed. Now, as we walk to school on our first morning back, we find most houses boarded up. Shutters closed. Doors locked. It looks like everyone's gone.

When it comes time for the school's roll call, the children line up in their class groups as they do every morning. Only now the lines are much shorter and there are gaps where entire classes used to be.

'Do you still have 150 students?' I ask the principal.

He winces. 'Officially, we have a hundred students enrolled but ...' he forces a smile and gestures to the playground. I do a quick head count as the students sing the national anthem. There are thirty-seven children here today.

That night, we sit around the fire with Aama, our little 'brother' Dhaney and our younger 'sister', Kashi, who is now pregnant with her first child. We drink *chiya* from chipped Nescafé mugs and stumble through the crumbled graveyard of our Nepali vocabulary, trying to catch up on three years of news. We hadn't spoken a word to each other since the day we left the mountain.

The family regale us with stories of the twenty-odd wacky and wonderful foreign volunteers the NGO sent to the village after us. There was the one who didn't shower or wash his clothes for a month until the smell became unbearable ... the one who fell down a ladder, then freaked out when the family sprinkled cold water on her face to see if she was conscious ... and the professional teacher who whipped the village kids into line after they locked her in the library, and became legendary on the mountain for teaching herself to play the Nepali violin.

Despite all their quirks and unusual ways, Aama concludes with a smile that all the volunteers have been *ramro manche*. Good people.

'Sometimes they seem strange and I don't understand them,' Aama laughs. 'But they teach me about other countries and I like that I can explore the whole world without leaving my kitchen.'

11

The first time we open the library we generate a small stampede. It's the first time the padlock has come off the doors in months and the children in the playground sprint towards us shrieking 'LIIIIE-BERRRRRY!' Our partner NGO stopped sending volunteers to run the library last year and the teachers claim they're too understaffed to manage it themselves. Given there's still the same number of teachers but only a third of the students left, this is a bit hard to swallow.

In a flurry of excitement, the kids discard their bags and shoes at the door and race to the shelves where there is an eruption of pencils, paper, puzzle pieces and storybooks. Within a few minutes, the faded blue carpet is covered in laughing, chattering children.

There are some new faces but many of our core library-loving kids are still here. When we ask after the students who are missing, we find some have transferred to boarding schools in Pokhara to get a better quality education. Others have been pulled out by their families to work in the fields. A few are gone, but no one can tell us where.

As I stand back watching the familiar chaos of the library unfold around me, a tall girl appears at the door. I look up and smile at her and she walks towards me with a stern expression on her face.

'How are you, Laura Maya? Good?' She asks, her English forceful. 'How long you are stay in Sundara?'

Her face is familiar but it's the first time I've come across a student in the village who could put English words together in whole sentences.

'You remember me?' The girl suddenly becomes shy and tucks her chin into her shoulder. Slowly her cheeks lift into a smile and that's when I see her.

'Anisha!' I exhale a huge rush of air, a breath I've been holding since Kolkata. 'Your English! Wow! Amazing!' She's having more success stringing words together than I am.

'You remember my name!' Anisha beams and I reach out a hand to touch her tiny arm.

'Of course I remember your name, Anisha,' *You're the reason I'm here*, 'and I see you've worked hard in school since we left. Your English is so good!'

Pride flickers across the eyes of the child who never used to smile and we just stand there for a few moments, grinning at each other until it gets awkward.

12

We only plan to stay two weeks in the village. We want to spend some time with the family, fix the library's roof which we're told is leaking and make sure human trafficking is on everyone's radar. From here, we're heading to Myanmar and Thailand where there are new projects to embark on, beaches to lie on, cocktails to drink … But every night we sit around the fire chatting with the family about the challenges the community is facing, and their answers trigger a series of avalanches that seem to block every escape route out of the village. The biggest question is, of course, 'Where did everybody go?'

'There's no work here,' Aama laments. 'No money. No opportunity.'

Dhaney does his best to translate as Aama explains that everyone is leaving in search of a better life. The poorest families move to the city or overseas to find jobs and a stable income, and the families who can afford it leave to put their children into better schools. Some are lucky to find the opportunities they're seeking, but others have only found trouble.

A few months ago, the daughter of a respected and well-educated member of the community was intercepted at the Indian border by the anti-slavery organisation, Maiti Nepal. The young girl and her family all thought she was being chaperoned by a trusted 'uncle' to a well-paying job cleaning houses in Mumbai. However, her travel guardian was a human trafficker who was about to sell her into a brothel—just like Mukti and the girls I met in Kolkata.

Clearly, we were right to be worried—girls and young women *are* at risk but so, we discover, are the men. They're taking out exorbitant loans from moneylenders so they can pay recruitment agencies to find them a job in the Middle East. When they arrive in these rich desert cities, many find their passports confiscated. They're forced to work twelve-hour days, six or seven days a week, for as little as $200 per month. To get ahead of the crippling interest rates on their loans, many work themselves to death. Literally. Healthy young men are dropping dead from heart attacks and heat stroke every day in the Middle East because they can't afford not to.

Nepal has one of the highest unemployment rates in the world, so a bad job is better than no income at all—even if, by the United Nations' standards, these 'jobs' are classified as modern slavery. For every horror story the men hear of someone going missing or dying, they know five other guys who make enough money cleaning toilets at Qatar International Airport that they could buy their mum a television. These little luxuries scream a thousand times louder than a hundred cautionary tales.

With the mass exodus of men from the village, the burden falls to women to take on all the work the men used to do. And we're not just talking about taking out the rubbish once a week. The women are left to plant and harvest all the crops on their terraced farmland which will nourish their family year-round, while also taking care of the house, cooking meals *and* raising their children. Stretched beyond their limits, their farmland becomes overgrown and unmanageable, so the women move their families to the city in search of work themselves. All over the mountain we can see old fields of rice smothered by wildflowers, an ironic symbol of fertility and growth in a land barren of opportunity. Of the families left in the village, many parents have pulled their children out of school to help work the fields. Learning to read, write and do maths is not as urgent as putting food on the table, even if illiterate children grow into vulnerable adults who will also have fewer economic opportunities. And the cycle continues.

So that's where everybody went, spinning around in a tornado of poverty that ripped through the village, tore families apart and flung everyone off in different directions in search of better weather.

The next burning question is, 'What can be done to improve the situation?'

Over many fireside conversations, Aama tells us the community needs jobs. Money. Better education for their children. We're careful not to jump back on our 'white saviour' horse again so we ask Aama and the villagers to come up with some solutions that we can help support.

Long story short, we never make it to Thailand. There are no cocktails. A year later we're still in Nepal, co-founders of not one, not two, but *three* non-profit organisations: one each in France and Australia so we can legally fundraise in our own countries, and one in Nepal that can oversee our projects which now stretch beyond the village to support survivors of trafficking from Kathmandu to the country's most western district of Humla.

Along with Sundara's school development committee president, we meet with officials at the district education office and, over several cups of tea, negotiate a new library building and solar-powered internet connection for the school. When the building works are underway and we can see the government has kept their end of the deal, we offer to purchase some computers and pay for a librarian's salary for the first two years. With the education initiatives on track, we turn our focus to employment. The villagers come up with some ideas for micro-businesses they can run from home, and we help set the wheels in motion. Along with another volunteer, we arrange training in commercial bee breeding so the villagers can learn to produce honey in large enough quantities to sell. Next, we help eight families band together to build a village homestay aimed at giving travellers a genuine experience of rural life in Nepal. It takes a lot of hair-pulling and frustration (and a few rupees slipped under the table) to get all these projects off the ground, but we're slowly moving forward. We help them register with the Ministry of Tourism, create a listing on the online accommodation platform, Airbnb, and within a few months the first paying tourists stagger into the village, sunburnt and bewildered, just like we did all those years ago.

13

I never got a sense that our host family and the other villagers *didn't* trust or accept us until the moment I realised they *did*. Now that we've left and come back to the village a few times, true to our word, something has shifted. Instead of approaching us with curiosity or excitement, the locals barely give us a second look anymore. We've gone from being a weird novelty to just another boring old piece of furniture. Which is a good thing. The walls are coming down and they let us see their more vulnerable sides—their anguish when a family member gets into trouble abroad, their tears when a loved one passes away. Their lethargy after a sleepless night and a long day driving an ox through the fields. Their humanness. This is all helped along by our ever-improving Nepali skills. We're now what I would call 'caveman fluent', so we have a vocabulary of a few hundred words we can use to communicate, even if we can't quite string them together.

When we first arrived in the village, calling everyone by family names like mother and sister, fooled us into believing these relationships ran deeper than they actually did. But the longer we carry those labels, the more weight they seem to hold. When Kashi gives birth to a baby girl, Sristi, her first and long-awaited child, we offer the gift of paying for her primary and high school education so she has the best possible start in life. The family are so touched by our gesture that they respond by refusing to allow us to continue paying for food and accommodation in their home. I only realise our relationship has been transactional now that it isn't anymore. This new dynamic cements our place in their lives, not as visitors or paying guests, but actual members of their family. Aama no longer fights us when we insist on doing the washing up, and when I ask what else I can do to contribute to the household I'm given the task of sweeping the courtyard every morning with a broom they made from tiger grass. When I don't completely screw that up, Aama decides I'm ready to take on more responsibility in the house.

Apparently, it's time I become a *real* Nepali woman.

14

'You know, in Nepal, it's not uncommon that a man can find another woman if his wife can't give him a child,' Aama says casually while stirring the curry, then she shoots David and me a cheeky smile.

Everyone around the fire laughs, including me, because I'm *pretty* sure she's being playful, and I honestly don't know what to say to the local women anymore to help them understand I have no interest in having a baby. Now that our Nepali is good enough to engage in basic conversations, it seems every day someone in the village wants to grill me about why I don't have children.

'But we don't *want* a baby,' I try to explain to the village women. 'David and I have made a choice.'

'But you *need* a baby,' argues our neighbour.

'Why?' I push back.

'Because you're a woman!' comes the exasperated response.

The villagers all turn to each other in bewilderment. They're looking at me in the same way I look at flat-earthers.

Now Aama is making it her personal mission to save David's bloodline and solve the problem of my childlessness. To do that she needs more information, so she's launched a full-blown inquisition into how childrearing works in Western society.

'Are you telling me people in your country go to work to earn money, then they pay it to someone else to take care of their children?' Aama eyeballs me and I scrunch up my nose, unsure how my casual enquiry about the family's new buffalo has brought us to the subject of childcare and, once again, my neglected uterus.

'No wonder you don't want to have kids! That makes no sense. Why don't you just have one baby, give it to me and I'll raise it for you while you work. For free!'

I grin as a vision dances across my mind of Aama running after a little blond, blue-eyed toddler jabbering away in Nepali. We're three generations of women sitting around the fire on the mud-packed floor of Aama's smoky kitchen. Kashi massages her now eight-month-old daughter with warm baby oil as she lies cradled in her crossed legs, while Aama cooks a pot of white rice over the flames. Both women keep one eye on my clumsy hands as I fumble to shell the beans they hope will be ready in time for tonight's dinner. The metal bowl is resting in my lap amongst the awkward layers of *lungi* and petticoat which I've now started wearing. It's not exactly comfortable, but I'm hoping if I at least *look* a bit more like a Nepali woman then I can fake it till I make it.

'That's the difference here, Aama,' I point out. 'In Nepal, your whole family lives in one house: mum, baby, grandma, aunts, uncles, cousins. Everyone raises the children *together*. In our society, most people live separately, just the parents and the children in one house. One parent has to work so there is money coming in, while the other parent takes care of the children alone all day. It's lonely and it's stressful. Life is expensive so sometimes *both* parents need to work to get enough money for their house and food. When that happens, if the children are too young for school, they go to childcare.'

'With strangers?'

'Yes. Well, they're more like teachers.'

'So, to *earn* money, you have to *pay* money to other people to take care of your children?'

'Yes.'

Aama reaches for a splintered log and pushes it into the dwindling fire. Contemplating that idea for a moment, she lowers her head towards the smouldering twigs and lets out a long whistling breath to bring the flames back to life. They inherited land from their family, and this humble mud house was built with the hands of their entire village more than fifty years earlier. For generations, almost everything they've eaten has come from their lush, terraced fields and the sweat and grit of their own hard work. When their children come into the world, they cling to their mother's backs or stay with family and neighbours in the village until they're old enough to take care of themselves. The community is more self-sufficient than where we come from, and less reliant on money.

'What vegetables do you have in your garden?' Aama quizzes me.

I shake my head. 'We don't have any vegetables in our garden. We buy everything from the supermarket.'

'What's a supermarket?'

'It's like a giant marketplace but inside a big building.'

'Ehhh,' Aama lifts her chin and nods slowly. 'You work to pay for your house, your children *and* your vegetables? So your whole garden is just for your buffalo?'

'No!' I giggle, 'We don't have a buffalo!'

Aama's mouth cracks into a perplexed smile. 'Then where do you get your milk from?'

'The supermarket,' I wince. 'Most of us go to work to earn money so we can *buy* everything we eat and drink.'

'Do you even have a garden?' Aama asks.

'I don't, but many people do, yeah,' I say, as Aama digs a spoon into the fluffy white grains she harvested 100 metres from her house. Steam escapes towards the roof and she pulls the pot off the flame, raising her chin to the air.

'And what's in their gardens?'

I look straight into her eyes and bite down on the inside of my bottom lip, scanning my mind for an appropriate response.

Sure, I know a few people with fruit trees or a little veggie patch out the back, but all I can think about is my parents' garden with its eight-person jacuzzi, complete with underwater disco lights. Next to it is a decommissioned vending machine stocked with bottles of pre-mixed Jim Beam and Coke. I picture my sister's garden, with its palm trees and seven-metre swimming pool. Then I think of my mother-in-law's garden with a three-car driveway, rose bushes and one of those paranoid trampolines with the big nets and crazy padding, so kids can't bounce right off them like we used to in the nineties.

'Flowers,' I answer finally, 'and grass.'

'But why do you need grass if you don't have a buffalo to feed?' Aama waves her rice-covered spoon at me, exasperated.

I remember scorching summer days in my childhood when I stripped down to my undies and ran through an old copper sprinkler on the lawn. Or lazy Sunday afternoons in my twenties when I lay on the grass in the sunshine, hoping it would somehow soak up my hangover like a sponge. But telling Aama this is unlikely to help my case, so I draw a deep breath and sigh. 'Good question, Aama.'

Aama gives a playful smirk and reaches out to retrieve the dented metal bowl of beans I've finally finished shelling. The beans hiss and spit as she pours them into a charred saucepan of sunflower oil and, with a vigorous stir, she asks one final question I can't answer. 'So why have grass when you could plant vegetables?'

Checkmate. We all laugh and Aama gives a matter-of-fact nod in my direction. 'You see? You get rid of the grass and plant enough vegetables that you can eat some and sell the others. Now you don't need money to buy food and you can afford to stay home and take care of your own babies.'

It's an oversimplification of the issue but still, I can't argue with Aama's logic. Part of the reason I don't want to populate the planet is because our society seems to expect women to keep working as if they don't have kids and nurture their children as if they don't work. And I'm terrible at multitasking.

Now that communication is easier, Aama is hungry for answers to these questions about us that have been burning inside her for years. Whenever we explain something about life in France or Australia, she sits back on her heels and stares upwards, as if looking at images of our strange world unfolding in the sky.

By now, we know that Aama was born in a Gurung village on a different mountain and moved to Sundara when she married Baba as a teenager. She vaguely remembers visiting Kathmandu once but the furthest she tends to venture is the nearest city, Pokhara, where her daughters live. She sometimes attends festivals in town, goes to the temple or seeks treatment at the hospital, but these few places are the limit of her experience of the world. Within this safe and familiar bubble, without a television or the ability to read any books or newspapers, Aama can only imagine our society in the same way we might conjure up images of an alien planet. And we're the weird little green men.

15

Food, culture and family are inseparably linked in Nepal, so now Aama has made the connection between my barren womb and my barren (non-existent) garden, she tries to take a different approach. I'm not sure if it's to challenge or train me, but Aama starts giving me more responsibility in the kitchen. In addition to peeling and cutting beans and potatoes, she now leaves me to watch over the occasional cauldron of boiling milk or a sizzling pot of vegetable curry. These tasks are so simple in her mind but fill me with uncontrollable anxiety. I can cook basic meals for two people on a stovetop where you can regulate the heat with a button, but not dinner for a large Nepali family on a wild and unpredictable fire in the floor. The first time I'm left to survey the boiling buffalo milk, it bubbles over like a volcano and floods half the kitchen. I waste an entire day's labour in three seconds.

Either Aama believes in my potential or she's stubbornly determined for me to change, so she perseveres with my training and I carry on murdering her vegetables and burning her flatbread.

'One day,' Aama declares, waving her spoon in the air after I singlehandedly destroy a pot of rice that should have fed eight people, 'I will come to France and teach you how to cook rice like a proper Nepali woman!'

Aama laughs so hard at her own joke that her whole body

shakes. How would she ever get her hands on enough money to travel to the other side of the world so she could teach me how to be a better woman?

'Okay, Aama,' I nod my head. 'You can come to France and teach me to cook rice.'

Aama scoffs and turns back to the burnt pot to see if any rice can be salvaged. 'Imagine how much money I'd need to fly to France. I'd have to sell Baba!'

The whole family cracks up, including Baba, and our raucous laughter slices through the quiet Himalayan night. Aama lifts the bottom of the towel she has wrapped around her head like a scarf and dabs at her watering eyes, weeping at the hilarious idea of trading her husband for a trip to Paris.

As the laughter fades, I look over at David and raise my eyebrows. He gives me a little nod, permission to unleash words from my mouth that can never be taken back. Words that will change all our lives forever.

'Aama, if you want to go to France, we will take you.' I look Aama straight in the eye so she knows I'm serious.

The room falls silent and Aama's brow furrows. She almost smiles before she dismisses the idea completely.

'Don't be ridiculous!' She scolds me. 'Who would take care of the buffalo? And the house and fields? And Baba?'

'Kashi and your sons can take care of the buffalo, and Baba could come too,' David suggests.

'What would Baba do in France? He's deaf! He has no teeth. And he doesn't talk unless you give him *raksi*. He'd have to be drunk the whole time!'

Baba chuckles from the back of the room and shakes his head, amused but not entertaining the idea for a second. 'Not possible,' he points to his mouth and ears, then twists his hands between them both, a common gesture that means, 'It doesn't work'.

Truth be told, although we've offered, I can't see any way Baba can travel to Europe. At this point, we've been coming and going from the village for almost five years and our relationship with Baba is still the same as it was the day we met him. As soon as he wakes in the morning, he grabs his hook-shaped knife and heads for the fields. There is grass to cut for the buffalo, saffron to dig up and millet to harvest. On the odd occasion our paths cross during the day, we exchange no more than a mute smile and nod and carry on in separate directions. At night, with a drink in his hand, Baba comes alive, and David sometimes sits with him at the back of the room. Drunk, the two of them pretend to have a conversation, each taking turns to speak in their own languages without any idea what the other is saying. This makes us all laugh, but it's the limit of our ability to interact with Baba.

'You could come alone, Aama. Visit new places, try new food … You can learn about our culture like we've spent all these years learning about yours.'

'No, I can't. I'm too old.' Aama gives a defiant shake of her head, signalling that the conversation is over.

'Well, you think about it,' I concede, sitting back against the clay wall. 'If you want to go to France so you can see what life is like where we're from, David and I will pay for your plane tickets.'

16

I've often daydreamed about taking Aama to Europe so she can understand what life is like in our culture—and not just the supermarkets and kitchens with four electric burners where you can cook an entire meal in twenty minutes. I want to show Aama all the ways humans can break the mould of what might be considered acceptable in the village: like unwed couples with children, interracial marriages and men staying at home with the kids while mum goes to work. I would love for her to explore our systems for education, employment and entrepreneurship, not because they're better, but because they're *different*. Maybe it would spark some ideas or broaden her view of what's possible for her community. Because no matter how long we stay in the village, we're aware that we may never understand their culture and challenges enough to know how to help them in a lasting and meaningful way. And the villagers tend to come up with ideas for how to improve their situation within the scope of what they already know about the world. So I wonder what kind of impact it might have on the community if someone as powerful and well respected as Aama—the village chief who sits on every decision-making committee on the mountain—gets the chance to experience a different way of life. To explore people, places, foods, customs, religions, landscapes, technology and *opportunities* unlike anything she's ever seen before. Not only that but couldn't Aama do with a holiday? After sixty-three years of tireless work raising her family, tending her fields and supporting her community, didn't this warrior woman deserve a break? To have someone take care of her so she can keep taking care of everyone else.

I'd daydreamed about taking Aama on a trip like this but never given it serious thought until the day I went into a second-hand bookshop in the city. I'd spent an hour skimming blurbs and moving piles of dusty books to find my next read, when a title leapt out at me: *Aama in America.* In the 1970s, a Peace Corp volunteer, Broughton Coburn, went deep into the Himalayas to live with Vishnu Maya, an elderly Gurung woman who belongs to the same ethnic group as Aama and Baba. In the 1980s, when Vishnu Maya was eighty-four and 1.4 m tall, Broughton and his Nepali Aama travelled to the United States for eight weeks on a trip encouraged by her village priests as a way to earn merit by making a difficult journey later in life.

This reverse cultural exchange had been done before.

I read the book in two sittings and passed it on to David, who was already on board with the idea. After the sale of her house, Véronique had generously given us some money to invest in something sensible like a home or a business. Or a baby. Instead, we could use it to take Aama on a life-changing journey and offer Véronique an unforgettable early sixtieth birthday present by bringing her Nepali 'sister' to her Normandy home. It was decided, then, without a huge amount of thought or forward planning, that if Aama wanted to visit France, we would make it happen. But for now, it seems she's not interested.

We don't push the idea but I can tell it's playing on Aama's mind. Whenever I screw up one of my chores—which happens less and less as my kitchen training pays off—Aama flashes a cheeky grin and tells me she'll come to France to teach me how to do it properly. Then she laughs and dismisses the idea for any one of a hundred different reasons that her travelling to Europe is impossible.

No one Aama knows has ever done anything like this before so it feels like it can't be done. Her sons have left the farm to go work in the Middle East and send their money home, but she's never known another Nepali soul to travel to the other side of the world, with no money to their name, for no other purpose than *exploration.* Not to mention that she would be placing her life in the hands of a malnourished white woman who doesn't even know how to cook rice.

One afternoon, months later, David and I are sitting in the courtyard, soaking up the winter sunshine while Aama and Kashi bustle around us, preparing the evening meal. I'm sitting cross-legged on a large straw mat, chopping cauliflower with a blunt kitchen knife while David lies next to me reading the final pages of *Aama in America.* An image of the eighty-four-year-old woman in traditional Gurung dress beams from the front cover. She is looking up at the bright lights of Times Square in New York with a wistful, toothless smile. David puts the book down on the mat while we chat, and the familiar sight of the Gurung woman on the cover catches Aama's eye.

'What's that?' Aama squats down on her haunches and picks up the book.

'It's the story of an American volunteer who took his Nepali

Aama to America,' says David, and Aama's eyes bulge.

'But this is a Gurung woman,' Aama splutters, touching the face of the tiny, hunchbacked woman on the book, 'and she's really old!'

'She's eighty-four. And she went to America thirty years ago!' I grin.

'But I'm only sixty-two! Or maybe sixty-three,' Aama says, 'and Baba is only seventy-eight! And I can't see for sure, but this tiny woman might not have a lot of teeth!'

As Aama studies the book, all the excuses for why she and Baba can't come to France start melting away.

'Ehhh. If this old Gurung woman could go wandering abroad then so can we, right?' Aama looks at each of us in turn and we nod with enthusiasm.

'Okay, David. Laura Maya. Take us to France.'

17

It's only when we fill out the forms to apply for Baba's passport that we realise no one in the family knows how old he is. Not even Baba. He owns just two official pieces of identity, and they place his birthday two years apart. Aama's birthday is clear, but we run into a hurdle when we're told she needs to be jewellery-free in her passport photo. Like many older Gurung women, Aama's twenty-odd gold earrings are soldered into her ear lobes and can only be removed with bolt cutters. However, the clerk tells us if we don't want the passport application to be rejected, we should visit the entrepreneurial gentleman in the makeshift booth outside the passport office who will photoshop them off her face for a dollar. Miraculously, both passports are issued, with two years shaved off Baba's life and Aama looking a bit like Dr Spock.

The French Embassy in Kathmandu asks for so many documents to accompany their visa application I wonder if they're going to use them to create a magical pathway all the way to Paris. They want birth certificates, marriage certificates and school certificates for two people who were born, married and educated (or not) in villages still cut off from the world today. And they want them in *French*. This is why in France we often refer to public administrators as 'papivores'. Like carnivores who eat paper.

With the application ready, Aama and Baba make the four-day return journey to Kathmandu to scrawl their names on one piece of paper at the visa processing centre. Aama's names are the only words she knows how to write, and the pen looks awkward and uncomfortable in her hand. Then Aama and Baba take the next bus out of Kathmandu to escape the heaving, honking stench of the city and return to Sundara to await the outcome of their visa application. A week later, an official from the French Embassy calls David to accuse him of refugee smuggling. He says we've taken no care at all to disguise the fact that Aama and Baba are planning to overstay their visa and seek asylum in France. David gets flustered and argues that we don't even live in France, that we need Aama and Baba here in Nepal where *we* live with *them*, but the arrogant diplomat hangs up on him.

18

It seems the adventure is over before it's even started, but we don't have time to agonise over the outcome because another cultural exchange expedition is about to begin. It's kind of a test run for Aama and Baba's trip to France, but in reverse …

David's fun-loving father, Alain, and his bubbly wife, our 'bonus mum' Elena, have just arrived in Kathmandu from Paris. My father-in-law has brought a suitcase full of cheese and 'emergency' wine and he happily chats to everyone he meets in French, whether they understand him or not. We've travelled a lot with Alain and Elena over the years and we always have a great laugh together, so we're excited to welcome them on their first trip to Nepal. But summer is a difficult time to travel in the Himalayas, when the earth and sky meet in the teeming monsoon, and things aren't quite going as well as we hoped. Sundara village lies on a similar latitude to Baja California in Mexico and the Canary Islands in Spain. It's a tropical climate at high altitude where in the winter months we have clear skies every day and feel uncomfortably close to the sun. However, at this time of year, the Himalayas that tower over the village are invisible for months, hidden by clouds that reach all the way down to fluorescent green fields alive with fiery red dragonflies. There are only two seasons in Sundara: the cold season and the hot season. Also known as the dry season and the wet season. Or the season when the village can be accessed by road, and the season when it cannot. So now, it's hot and wet and the road to the village has washed away. Alain and Elena's first introduction to Sundara is a gruelling five-hour trek through a raging river and up a mountain in the humid, blistering heat. Tempers flare and what transpires that morning is the worst of love and travel. At one point, half of us throw our sweaty, swollen bodies into the ice-cold river, desperate to cool off with an almost audible sizzle. All of us, at some stage of the journey, admit defeat and declare the only logical thing to do now is return to the hotel in Pokhara with the cocktails and the pool.

When we eventually stagger into Aama and Baba's courtyard, Alain and Elena look flustered and exhausted. And shocked. They've seen plenty of photos of the house before, but its rustic simplicity can only be fully appreciated when you're towering above the kitchen door like a giant. Aama emerges from the house to greet them with an enormous smile and, we notice, sporting a whole new look. Meeting the father of her chosen son for the first time is an important moment. Aama has pulled her hair back tight into a fresh braid, red wool plaited through so it hangs down to her lower back. Her usual baggy, tattered woollen vest, covered in practical pockets full of tools and treasures, has been replaced with a thin, sleek grey cardigan that hugs her body. She's also wearing a fresh *lungi*. Her entire outfit is so new that the creases where the clothes were folded in the packet are still lightly visible.

'Welcome to our home,' Aama greets Alain and Elena, gently placing a white ceremonial scarf around their sunburnt necks. Elena beams and gushes her gratitude, but my normally jovial father-in-law struggles to force his frown muscles into reverse.

'He's tired,' I try to explain away his stunned, flustered expression. 'It was a difficult climb up the hill in the heat.'

Aama waves her hand at him and cackles, 'Yes, it's a little difficult to get to my house in the monsoon season!' As if the two-day journey from Kathmandu in the dry season is a stroll through the cherry blossoms.

'*Oui!* I almost died!' Alain's sense of humour returns. With his fingers he mimes someone walking up lots of steps then lets his head fall to the side with his tongue sticking out, pretending to be dead. Everyone laughs and the tension is broken. Aama nods, points a finger at Alain's well-nourished belly and puffs out her cheeks to make herself look fatter.

'Yes, with a belly like yours, you should come in the winter,' Aama states with a matter-of-fact nod. 'When you're carrying extra baggage it's better to take the bus!'

19

We're supposed to stay in the village for another two days but when we wake the following morning, Alain has decided to return to the city. Last night, the thin foam mattress on Alain's wooden bed gave his injured back about as much support as a sponge cake. And even if he did have a proper mattress, it was impossible to sleep with the torrential rain coming down on the tin roof like a thousand steel drums at a military tattoo. With his chronic back pain and high blood pressure exacerbated by the oppressive humid heat, Alain physically cannot stay in the village for another day.

This puts David and me in a lose–lose position. For Aama, if Alain leaves early, it means he's not comfortable or happy in her home, so she will feel offended and ashamed. For Alain, staying in the village to avoid hurting Aama's feelings will result in a deterioration of his health, which means it will be harder for him to make the long trek back to the city. It's no one's fault but, either way, someone we care about is going to be upset.

I wait until there's no one else around to join Aama by the fire and try to explain all of this to her gently. She winces when she hears the news and reaches for a spoon, turning her face towards the flames. Then she stirs the curry silently, trying not to cry.

'I promise it has nothing to do with you, Aama,' I lean in, trying to catch her eye. 'He loves it here and he's so happy to meet you. I know it's hard to understand now but … he comes from a different world.'

A world with tiled roofs and skylights, instead of tin. Where the rooms are air-conditioned and temperature controlled, not humid and billowing with smoke from the kitchen fire. A luxurious place where people can and do spend more money on a memory foam mattress than they would on a car. But these are all impossible concepts to explain to Aama now, before she's seen any of it herself.

It's a sombre departure from the village. Aama smiles and puts on a brave face, knowing she's given Alain and Elena the best of everything she has but it still wasn't enough. This is the first inkling we get that this whole France–Nepal cultural exchange project might be a spectacularly bad idea. If Aama and Baba's response to France is like Alain's experience in the village, it might be better if they *don't* get the visa. Maybe we've been in Nepal for so long that we've become blind to all the ways these cultures are so different. It's possible Aama and Baba will have the same strong reaction when they see how we live. Maybe their backs won't cope with soft beds, their stomachs won't process such rich food and the blustery cold Normandy weather will make them weak and sick. At least now Alain and Elena can retreat to a Western-style hotel in Pokhara with all the familiar mod cons of home, but if Aama and Baba struggle to cope in Paris, where do we go? Now I wonder if the grumpy embassy official who accused us of people smuggling may actually have done us a favour.

That's why I struggle with mixed emotions when we collect the passports in Kathmandu and discover he granted them a thirty-day visa for Schengen Europe after all. When we call to tell Aama the news, her voice cracks with emotion and she beams, 'Very, very, very *merci!*' It's one of the only words she knows in French and she's been practising.

Now that we have the green light, we move from the

dreaming to the planning phase. Emails fly around the world to the Netherlands, Ireland, Italy and France, informing friends and family of our impending arrival. As the blank spaces on our calendar start filling up, the reality of what we're embarking on creeps over me.

We're taking two indigenous elders from the only home they've ever known in a remote Himalayan community and travelling with them to Paris. They've spent most of their lives in a village that didn't have electricity or even a road. They've never seen hot water come out of a tap. They don't know how to use a knife and fork. They've never been on a plane or boat or driven on a freeway. They don't even know how to use a seated toilet or toilet paper. How are we going to communicate with them beyond our caveman-style 'Nepali village' vocabulary? How will we explain to them how to live in our world? What are they going to think when they see us pay the equivalent of a week's salary in Nepal for one meal in France? After they see how big and opulent our houses are? And what the hell is Baba going to eat with only three teeth?

I guess we're about to find out.

20

There is a quiet chaos brewing when we return to the village. We have two days left to prepare for our trip and Aama is darting around the house in a frantic panic, trying to get everything done.

'There's so much work and no one here to do it!' Aama wails when we settle around the fire for dinner. 'I thought my sons would be here to take care of the house while we're gone but now none of them are coming. How is Kashi going to cope with the house and the fields and Sristi all on her own? And who will look after my tomatoes? *Ke garne? Ke garne? …*'

This common Nepali expression, which means 'What to do?', normally feels calming and philosophical when someone says it. Like, 'What can we do about it now? Nothing? Oh well! Let's just move on then. *Ommmmmmm.*' But as *ke garne* tumbles from Aama's lips now, she's definitely got more of a 'hyperventilating into a paper bag' thing going on.

'Don't worry,' I tell Aama as she channels her anxiety into the four cloves of garlic she's pummelling between two stones. 'This is normal before you travel. Everything feels like a problem before you leave, but then you go and somehow it's all okay. You'll see.' Aama raises her eyes to look at me but says nothing as she pounds the garlic to a pulp.

Neither Aama nor I sleep much that night and I hear her bustling around the courtyard at three in the morning as I start to drift off.

When I stumble into the kitchen four hours later with my eyes still half crusted shut, pillow marks carved into my face, I find Aama alone by the fire, sipping a cup of tea.

'Not much sleep?' I ask.

Aama waves a dismissive hand at me. She lifts the Thermos

and strains some *chiya* into a Nescafé mug, then places it on the dirt floor in front of me. 'I was awake all night worrying.'

I clutch the mug to my chest, hoping I'll find my sanity at the bottom. I want to be encouraging and tell Aama everything is going to be alright, but I'm not convinced of that myself anymore. I don't want to force her to take this trip if she's not ready. If none of us is ready. 'You know Aama, if you don't want to come to France this time ... if it's too difficult ... it's okay. We can go next year when you feel more prepared.'

'*Hoina!*' Aama waves me off, rejecting the idea. 'We told everyone on the mountain we're going to Europe. If we don't go now, what will people say?'

'We'll tell them there was a problem with the plane,' I wink.

'*Hoina!*' Aama fights back again. 'Yes, we have problems to work out before we go but if we wait until next year, there will just be other problems. I'm *terrified*. But if we don't go now, I'll have too much time to think about it and we'll never go at all.'

'So, we're going to France?'

'We're going to France,' Aama says with a nod of false confidence.

It's astonishing how easily problems can be solved over a cup of tea in Nepal. Now we may need a second mug as I broach a more complicated subject.

'What time do you want to leave tomorrow?'

As a Gurung woman, Aama's personal religion borrows from both Buddhist and Hindu practices, some of which can lend itself to certain superstitions. It's important for Aama that this journey has an auspicious start, so we can't just up and go to Europe whenever we want without first looking at the corresponding numbers and stars. A week ago, we sat with a medicine woman and half a dozen villagers in Aama's kitchen to sort through which dates and times were ideal for embarking on such an adventure. David and I wanted to leave the village on Sunday 10 August, but there was a quiet uproar when we suggested this, as well as some impassioned discussions about a horse (of which there are none in the village). The date was unanimously dismissed. First, they had to determine *when* the journey begins. Is it the day we leave the village? The day we take the bus from Pokhara to Kathmandu? Or the day we fly out of Nepal? After much deliberation and enthusiastic nodding, the women agreed that Saturday 9 August at 10 am was the most auspicious time to start a journey to Europe.

Baba, on the other hand, chuckled throughout most of these discussions and seemed unfazed about the details. That night, as I'm crouched at the water source packing the clean copper plates into a straw basket, Baba sneaks up behind me. I startle and almost drop the basket when I turn around and find him standing there with a big goofy grin on his face.

'Just four more days,' Baba croaks, 'then—' he grins and his eyes pop open in delight. He throws his arms out to the sides like a pair of aeroplane wings and whooshes playfully around the moonlit courtyard.

'Are you excited, Baba?' I grin and yell towards his good ear. He stops to look at me, his face beaming, then he gives one deliberate nod before gliding away through a sky of imaginary clouds towards his bed.

This may be the closest thing to a conversation Baba and I have ever had.

21

When the auspicious day comes for us to start our journey to Europe, we're all awake with the sun, too excited to sleep.

I pop my head into the kitchen to find Aama, as expected, making rings of *sel roti*, a traditional 'someone's leaving the village' donut bread, over the fire.

'Do you need help packing?'

'It's done!' Aama points at a small cube-shaped shopping bag by the kitchen door, the kind used by Nepali villagers to transport vegetables, rice and the occasional baby goat.

'That's it?' My eyebrows reach skyward. 'That tiny bag? For both of you?'

'Our suitcase is in Pokhara but yes, that's all we need,' Aama shrugs.

'You have a change of clothes in there?'

'Two *lungi*, two T-shirts and two saris for me. Two pants, two shirts and a waistcoat for Baba.'

'Ah, don't you think you should maybe take three of everything? At least?'

Aama looks at me, confused. 'We can only wear one set of clothes at a time, can't we?'

'Well, yes, but …'

'When we put the clean clothes on, we wash the dirty ones so they're clean again. Why do we need more than that? I've only got one body!' Aama laughs. She thinks I'm joking.

By most French and Australian standards, David and I are minimalists. I have condensed my life to the 23 kg I travel with, and everything I own of value fits in a faux-leather handbag I bought for $4 in Thailand. Now, next to Aama, I feel like a hoarder. I want to argue they should bring one extra set of clothes—just in case something happens—but I can't disagree with her logic. She does only have one body. We all do.

'Are you sure you have everything you need in there? Medication? Shoes?' I ask as we move outside.

'Yes, and some honey I can give to Véronique *bahini*,' Aama continues, holding up an old Coca Cola bottle to the light so we can see all the sticky, dead baby bees entombed inside. David and I exchange a quick glance before he tries to explain she can't bring her honey to France.

'Why not?' Aama explodes, scrunching up her face in defiance. 'It's good honey! Made in my brand-new hive!'

A crowd of villagers have gathered at the house to see Aama and Baba off, and now they're staring at David in shock. We try to explain international customs and quarantine laws using our farmyard Nepali but when that fails, David keeps it simple, 'If you pack the honey, the airport police will stop you and take it away.'

'No problem!' Aama laughs, tucking the honey under her woollen vest. 'When I see the airport police, I'll just hide it under my shirt like this.' She buries the Coca Cola bottle under her armpit and shuffles past us with an exaggerated and innocent smile. 'I'll just walk like this and say to them, "No, no, I don't have anything," and of course they'll let me through. How will they know?'

She'll remember this conversation a few days later when her entire body is X-rayed and she gets a full pat down by a perfect stranger at Kathmandu airport, but for now she gives a triumphant nod and drops the honeybee graveyard in the bag with her two pairs of clothes.

When the clock strikes ten, an excited buzz emanates from the crowd of villagers who have gathered to wish Aama and Baba a safe journey. The farewell ceremony begins and Kashi approaches me holding a copper tray of red powder. She presses the *tika* onto our foreheads then drapes garlands of fresh flowers and silk scarves around our necks.

I thought leaving home might be a difficult and emotional moment for Aama and Baba, but instead it's filled with laughter and joyful anticipation. The villagers are giggling with excitement and a large crowd swells around us.

We're about to leave when, out of the corner of my eye, I see Kashi feed something into Aama and Baba's mouths. Before I understand what's happening, she turns to me next and makes a beeline for my face with a spoon full of white goop.

'Don't!' Aama yelps. 'Laura Maya doesn't like—'

Aama tries to leap between the spoon and my mouth like a goalie but it's too late. The metal hits my tongue and I gag violently as the warm, sour milk trickles down my throat.

'Ugh. Why?' I scrunch up my face, eyes watering.

'Because you're going on a journey, sister,' Kashi explains, as if that somehow answers my question.

'But why a spoonful of milk? What does that do?'

All the villagers look to each other for a response but no one has one.

Kashi turns back to me and giggles, 'I don't know, sister. When someone leaves on a big trip, that's just what we do.'

It baffles me that this is the response I get to so many of my cultural questions in Nepal. Once when I asked, 'Why is the school closed tomorrow, Aama?' she responded, 'It's a public holiday. Something to do with a snake. Or sugarcane. I can't remember. All I know is it's marked in red on the calendar, so everything is closed.'

There are over a hundred days marked in red on the Nepali calendar. Their culture is rich with religious and cultural traditions, but I can't understand why they perform these rituals without ever asking themselves why.

Right before we leave, Kashi crouches down to the ground in front of Aama and touches her feet. Unlike the milk, this is a ritual I've seen many times before, usually when Kashi leaves the village to visit her family for a few days. I've never asked the meaning behind it, but watching it always makes me uncomfortable so I look away. It doesn't sit right with me that a daughter-in-law, a subordinate, crouches to touch the feet of the matriarch who rules the household, as if she is lower in status somehow. Positioned as a daughter-in-law in the family myself, I wonder if this is something they expect me to do, too. But I figure if I never ask, I'll never know, and I'll never need to wrestle with the internal conflict of having to bow at anyone's feet.

Now it seems everyone on the mountain has gathered to witness this historic event: Dar Kumari and Nar Bahadur Gurung, whose lives rarely stretch beyond this mountain, are travelling to Europe. The villagers laugh and pat our backs as we pass their homes. Sometimes they pull us in for a quick sideways hug and press flowers into our hands before joining the swell of people who escort us to the gateway of the village— to the same place where we parted ways with Aama all those years ago, when I promised to return.

From there, Aama and Baba skip down the hill at a lightning pace, barrelling confidently down this well-worn path of their comfort zone, their last familiar steps before leaping into a gaping unknown.

22

We arrive at Kathmandu airport at 6 am on 12 August. The noise outside the departure terminal sounds like a thousand people calling the final length of a horse race, all at the same time. When we emerge from our car, we're absorbed into the cacophony, a bulging crowd of nervous and excited young Nepali men who are leaving to work abroad. Only passengers are allowed into the airport and the heaving, jostling queue to have our tickets checked feels a bit like a mosh pit. We link arms with Aama and Baba so we don't get separated, and this draws some curious stares from the people smooshed around us.

Apart from the grip we have on each other, we definitely don't look like we should be travelling together. Aama and Baba have busted out their fanciest clothes for this momentous trip to Paris. Baba is looking sharp in a brand-new tweed waistcoat, suit pants and a crisp white buttoned shirt, and Aama is wearing her wedding sari. It's the first time I've ever seen her not wear a *lungi* and she looks beautiful but not exactly comfortable. Swaddled in six metres of strategically tucked and billowing floral chiffon, all I can see is the disaster waiting to happen when she encounters her first super-suction aeroplane loo. Aama only learnt how to use a flush toilet for the first time less than twenty-four hours ago. Add half a dozen metres of flowing fabric and what could possibly go wrong?

Next to Aama and Baba, David and I look like a pair of proper Aussie bogans—baggy pants, faded T-shirts, shoes still covered in mud from our last trek through the river from the village. Aama and Baba are a picture of distinguished elegance, yet still every airport guard we encounter barks at them to back away from *us*, two wrinkled slobs being treated like VIPs just because we're tourists.

Tribhuvan International is a drab, brown brick building which looks a bit like an airport dressed up as a bus station. Here, it's not unheard of to encounter a flight delay if the national airline needs to sacrifice a couple of goats on the runway to appease the Hindu sky gods before take-off. There are no conveyor belts in the departure terminal, so our bags are loaded onto trolleys and pushed out to the plane by a baggage handler. The most cutting-edge technology in the airport is one lonely upwards escalator that transports passengers to the immigration hall. And this escalator is the first major hurdle between Aama and Baba and the Western world.

Their feet are anchored to the floor as they stand in front of the giant, moving staircase for a full minute without saying a word. Together, we watch the flat, crinkle-cut metal rectangles appear from the ground then morph into prisms, forming a zigzag that moves towards the sky. Self-conscious, Aama reaches for the bundles of chiffon around her legs and looks around for another staircase. One that doesn't move.

I can't blame them if they don't trust us to step onto the escalator at this point, not after everything we've told them over the last few days. Back in Pokhara we sat down with Aama and Baba's children and grandchildren and had 'the talk'. With their granddaughter Sunmaya as our translator, we spent several hours explaining to them all the things that might be shocking or troublesome for them in Europe. Like having to kiss everyone they meet once on each cheek. Or seeing women almost naked in bikinis on the beach. We covered racism, gender equality, homosexuality and animal rights, which all led to the grand finale of theoretical toilet training. This resulted in a long, confused discussion about why on earth we would smear our poo remnants around our anuses with toilet paper, chaffing ourselves clean with a non-renewable resource, when we could just wash ourselves with a cool splash of water.

In the face of all this new information we've asked them to trust us, but we also just asked them to hand over everything they own to a total stranger at the check-in desk. And now we expect them to risk their lives on rolling staircase?

'How do I get onto it,' Aama asks, her question directed to the escalator, 'without falling on my face?'

'Just take one step,' David motions for Baba to join him at the base of the escalator. He takes a firm grip on Baba's arm and hovers the other hand over the railing. Then he yells into Baba's ear, 'On the count of three take one step forward, okay?'

On three, David steps onto the escalator, pulling Baba with him. Baba wobbles as the stairs rise, one leg swinging to the side before David places a strong arm on his back to steady him. It's far more physical contact than Baba usually allows, but he looks up at David with a big toothless grin and a delighted, wheezing chuckle.

When they reach the top without falling to their death, Aama agrees to go next. As we rise up the escalator, her face is full of all the emotion and triumph of an Olympian on the winner's podium. I'm not too concerned about holding onto her because she's got a fistful of my knuckles in a crushing grip. A memory flashes in my mind of Aama snapping a corn cob in half with her bare hands in the village. Suddenly, I become so preoccupied with restoring the blood circulation to my hand that I forget she has no idea what to do when we reach the top.

I assume Aama will step off the escalator just as she stepped on, and she assumes I'll tell her if she needs to do something to avoid breaking her face. So, when we approach the top, she just looks down at her feet, still chuffed with herself, awaiting further instruction. I step forward alone and Aama trips and catapults into the immigration hall. She's still got my hand in a death grip so I swing around to catch her and somehow put her back on her feet without either of us toppling over. Around us, travellers and security guards, who had been watching the whole process with amusement, now all erupt into thunderous applause.

23

'*Ah ma ma*, what is happening here?'

We've entered the immigration hall where hundreds of young Nepali men are queued in a giant human snake that fills half the room. They're all covered in ceremonial scarves, red *tika* marking their foreheads, and shuffling towards several desks marked 'Work Migration'. On the other side, there are two short queues marked 'Tourists' and 'Other', with only three people in each. The room is so unbalanced it almost seems to be tilting sideways, as if the left side of the hall, like this country, is buckling under the weight of losing thousands of its men each day.

We move towards the empty 'Other' queue, the only logical place for our motley crew, and the immigration officer motions for us to approach the desk. As our group of four walks towards him he stands from his chair and starts waving both hands at

Aama and Baba.

'Go back, Aama!' he yells. 'The tourists were here first. Your turn will come next.'

'No,' I raise a stern hand to interrupt him, 'we're travelling together.'

His eyes widen and he looks around, searching for the candid camera.

Soon there are five gregarious, official-looking men gathered around us, all wearing suits and *topi,* and flaunting their staff IDs, lanyards of power adorning their necks.

Not for the first time since leaving the village, Aama and Baba find themselves at the centre of some uncomfortable attention. Everyone we've encountered, from taxi drivers to random strangers on the street, fire questions at Aama and Baba about who we are and why we're all together. But Aama always deflects these enquiries with striking composure and indifference. I can't tell if she's aloof because she's insulted or intimidated by these enquiries, or if she has a quiet self-confidence because she knows it's none of their business.

But these immigration agents aren't letting Aama and Baba fob them off with a vague explanation, and they have the authority to refuse their exit from Nepal if they're not satisfied with their responses. David and I explain as best we can that we're just a group of friends from different countries, travelling to France together for a holiday. When we speak in Nepali, the men laugh until they can barely breathe. Their raucous hysteria captures the attention of everyone in the immigration hall until all eyes in the 'Work Migration' snake are fixed on us.

'How are you funding this trip?' the immigration officer asks Aama and Baba.

'We're helping them,' David chimes in.

'They've done so much for us over the years, we just want to return the favour,' I add with a smile. The immigration officers murmur among themselves in hushed tones, shuffling through the reams of paperwork we've laid out before them to support our case.

'Aama!' one of the men becomes serious, addressing Aama directly so we cannot answer for her. He fixes her gaze, and she seems tiny and vulnerable looking up at him on his official perch. 'Tell me how you know these people. What is the reason for your trip to France?'

There's something in his tone that unnerves me. My heart pounds in my ears as it occurs to me, a bit like prey in the slow squeeze of a boa constrictor, that David and I might be under suspicion. *Two comparatively rich foreigners giving money to a couple of Himalayan farmers so they can go on a holiday? In what world is that a believable scenario?* Somehow, despite all my work in the modern abolition movement, I completely overlooked how this situation might appear to an immigration officer. A nervous giggle threatens to snort out my nose as I realise, with great irony, what's going on here.

Maybe he thinks I'm a human trafficker.

Still, Aama's face gives nothing away. She leans forward and responds in her lowest frequency voice so only the men in front of her can hear and the hundreds of people staring at us will have to die curious.

'They came to my house for the first time five years ago. Since then, they have come and gone many times. They built a library for our school. They set up home businesses in our village so we have money coming in. They live with us and we've become close. Like family. We teach them our ways and our culture so they understand what life is like in Nepal. Now they've offered to take us to Europe so we can learn about their culture and what life is like in their country. It's my first ever holiday.'

The immigration officer and Aama engage in a brief, silent staring competition as he pauses to consider his next move.

'This is your first time in Europe?' he breaks his silence.

'It's my first time on a plane,' Aama beams at him, 'and I'm *really* excited!'

The group of men return her smile warmly, even though she's said nothing that proves we're not planning to sell her into slavery.

'Have a safe journey, Aama.' The men tilt their heads from side to side, stamp our passports and send us on our way. Grateful, we all tilt our heads sideways in response and the men stand to wave at us as we officially leave Nepal.

PART 2

Qatar & France

The simple things are also the most extraordinary
things, and only the wise can see them.
—*Paulo Coelho, The Alchemist*

24

'I get my own TV,' Aama says, pointing at the tiny screen in the seat in front of her, 'but I have to be tied up like a buffalo?'

'Something like that,' David chuckles and reaches over to help Aama fix her seatbelt. He presses the two shining silver pieces towards each other and when she hears a loud click Aama looks up at David and grins.

'It's beautiful.'

So far everything about the aeroplane is beautiful. The seat covers, the tray tables, the no smoking signs … Aama and Baba are in a delirious trance. With great reverence, they reach out to touch everything they encounter as if it's sacred, including the tarmac, the emergency lights on the floor and the outline of the enormous letter Q that spells Qatar Airways on the side of the plane. Each time Aama touches something on this enormous metal bird, she then brings her fingertips to her head and mutters the same words under her breath. All I catch is '*bagawan jasto*'. Like gods.

When the pilot fires up the engines, a thunderous roar pulsates through the cabin. Baba starts to chuckle, but every muscle in Aama's delighted smile goes limp as the plane starts barrelling down the runway. The g-force pins her to her seat and she squeezes her eyes shut, repeating the same mantra, '*Ah ma ma ma ma*', in a quiet, frightened voice. The colour in her face drains a little. Her eyes dart back and forth to look at us and the other passengers. She's trying to understand if this is normal or if we're all about to die, so I flash her an over-the-top fake smile that I hope will both reassure her and mask the fact that I'm petrified of flying myself. Baba is hysterical at this point, but I can't tell if he's laughing because he's freaking out or if he's just enjoying the thrill of all his dreams coming true. David reaches out a comforting hand to Aama as the metallic wheels scrape off the runway and the plane takes flight. As the aircraft climbs into the sky, the cabin shudders. Terrified, Aama pokes her tongue right out, her eyes bulging as wide as eyes can go.

We watch the ground beneath us zoom past the window. The buildings, cars and people shrink and soon we're soaring over green, undulating hills that melt into the white peaks of the Himalayas. The pilot banks into the clouds, chasing the sun, then the plane levels out in an endless void of cornflower blue. The beautiful seatbelt sign switches off, Aama pulls her tongue back into her mouth and Baba sighs and rests his head back against the seat. I suspect the only reason he agreed to this madcap adventure was the chance to experience flying in an aeroplane and he's now wearing the satisfied smile of a man who can die with no regrets.

It's the first time in their lives they have had their own personal television to watch with dozens of channels, but they're more intrigued by the rolling meadow of white, fluffy clouds beneath them. They barely move or take their eyes off the window for the four hours we're in the air. When we land in Doha, we don't think to warn Aama and Baba to brace themselves and Aama's body flails forward, bending at the seatbelt as the plane hurtles towards the earth at 240 kph. Now she's grateful to be tied up like a buffalo.

Soon we're zooming through Hamad International Airport, being transported to our gate on golf carts in a high-speed convoy. Aama and I are on the back of the leading golf cart and David and Baba are on the back of the other. Every time the driver brakes, Aama lurches forward and threatens to somersault into the path of her husband's oncoming vehicle. She's giggling too hard to hold on, so I'm now gripping *her* arm like *I'm* trying to snap a corn cob and clinging to the metal bar above so we don't fall off.

'It's so new,' Aama breathes as we glide between crystal walls and over glistening white tiles. Thousands of glittering lights bounce off the sheets of glass that stretch from the carpet to the skylit ceiling. All around us, people are travelling at superhuman speeds, shooting up mirrored elevators and striding along moving footpaths. 'Everything here is huge and moves so fast! Nepal is so old and slow and small and dirty by comparison. This place is shining like diamonds.' I don't know the Nepali word for diamonds but Aama points to her fingers where those gems might be if she had been born into a different life.

25

'What are all these black things?'

We're watching the world go by as we wait for our flight to Paris. Aama's eyes follow the passengers as they pass by, some wandering through the airport and browsing in shops, while others are in a panic, sprinting towards their final boarding call.

Like a lot of older women in the village, Aama never points with her fingers but instead purses her lips together, raises her chin and make a silent kiss towards the object of her interest. In this case, the 'black things'. A group of figures draped in loose, dark fabric.

'They're women.'

'What?!' Aama straightens her back. 'Why are they hiding under those blankets?'

'It's part of their culture and religion. You are Gurung and a Buddhist and you wear a *lungi* most days. These women are Muslim and they wear a *niqab*. They have other clothes underneath but they cover themselves in these robes when they leave the house.'

'Are the men covered in black blankets too?'

'No,' I smile gently, 'only the women.'

'But how do they breathe in there?'

'I don't know,' I admit. I had never really thought about it.

'It would be hot in there,' Aama muses, staring at the women. 'It must be difficult for these women, don't you think?'

'Because it's hot?'

'No, because these women, when we look at them, we can't tell if they're happy or sad, can we?'

'That's true.' I steal a sideways glance at a group of veiled women sitting near us. We've been about a metre apart for a couple of hours and none of us have acknowledged each other, which is weird for me because I'm normally pretty chatty with strangers. David finds it unsettling that I can strike up a casual conversation with the person behind me in the supermarket checkout queue and by the time I'm fumbling for my wallet to pay for my groceries, I've uncovered all their lifelong dreams and the fears that are holding them back. But when a woman is wearing a *niqab*, there's a physical barrier between us and I realise now, despite transiting the Middle East a couple of times each year, I've never tried to cross it. Maybe because Aama's right—it's too hard to tell what kind of a day these women are having, or if they just want to be left alone. But now, as we embark on this epic intercultural adventure, it seems like a perfect opportunity to try and break down some walls.

'Hi there,' I call out in their direction with a smile that I hope comes off as warm and not too crazy.

'Hello,' the veiled women nod.

'Where are you travelling today?'

'Egypt,' one woman responds, her voice slightly muffled by the fabric.

One of the young girls in the group, whose face is not covered, flashes us a bright smile, 'We're going to Cairo.'

'Oh lovely. You have family there?' I push on, encouraged

by the girl's grin. Everyone in the group nods back at me. By the gentle creases around their eyes, I think they're smiling but I can't be sure. I nod to acknowledge their nods and the conversation ends.

Aama spends the next hour watching the women in the black cloth. A few times I open my mouth to suggest she looks away because it's rude to stare. But then I realise I have no idea if that's true in Nepali or Qatari culture, so I close it again.

26

I've lost track of how long we've been travelling but, based on how I feel right now, I estimate it's been about four and a half years. Aama rests her weary head against the aeroplane window but refuses to sleep because it's light outside. Instead, she presses her nose against the glass and fires questions at me that I'm too ignorant to answer.

'What's that place?'

'Maybe Saudi Arabia?'

'Ah that's where my son-in-law works. It just looks like sand. Is it all sand?'

'I think so, yes.'

'How do they get water?'

'Ummm …' I think back to my own experience staying at a camp in the Moroccan Sahara and scan my brain for any documentary I may have seen about people living in the desert. Nothing comes to me. We're well beyond the scope of my Nepali village vocabulary so I flick through the pocket dictionary to find the word for 'oasis'. When there isn't one, I settle on: tiny pond things.

So far, I haven't answered even one of Aama's questions with conviction but she's not giving up on me.

How much of the world is sand? And grass? And water? That much water, really? Why am I only seeing sand? Where are the grassy places? What country are we over now? Who lives there? What religion are they? Do they hide their women under blankets there, too?

Eventually, mid-sentence, Aama falls asleep. When she wakes up with a jolt an hour later, we're somewhere over Germany.

'Is it tomorrow?' Aama clears her throat and stares at her watch for a solid minute, blinking. It's two minutes to midnight in Nepal but the sun is still shining like it's lunchtime. 'It's midnight. Why is the sun still awake? It's been awake all day.'

Like most people living in communities with limited electricity, Aama is guided through her day by the sun, a natural clock. She wakes with the dawn, works through the daylight hours and doesn't rest until the sky is full of stars. If the sun is working, so is she. Now, exhausted, disoriented and awake way past her bedtime, Aama is searching for a star to tell her it's okay to close her eyes again.

I throw out every word I know in Nepali to try and explain the concept of time zones and the rotation of the earth, but nothing sticks.

'You see, we left the hotel in Kathmandu just after sunrise. The earth spins to the east. We're travelling to the west, so we're following the light.'

Aama blinks at me.

I pull out a pen and draw a diagram of the globe and sun on a napkin. Then I draw a tiny aeroplane and little dotted lines indicating the direction of travel and the rotation of the Earth.

'Are you joking?' Aama scrunches up her face.

'It's true!' I smile. She studies my face for a moment, unsure what to believe. I look back down at my diagram and see how— on reflection—it *does* look a bit like a butterfly on a basketball shooting lasers out of its bum. Neither of us know where to go from here, so we return our attention to the window television, where Aama sees even more new things that inspire questions I can't answer.

As the plane makes its approach to Paris, I point out the elusive grass she was searching for earlier. The forest canopies and fields of corn and mustard are a patchwork of green and yellow, divided by swirling grey roads. A satisfied smile spreads across Aama's face when she remains strong in her seat as the aircraft screeches and bumps along the runway before slowing to a crawl.

'We're in Paris, Aama,' I exhale. 'We made it.'

'Pariiis,' Aama breathes the word out. She lowers her head to look at the sky from the window. When she finds it's still a maddening shade of blue, Aama turns to me with a fierce, accusing look.

'Ok, enough! Tell me why the sun shines all day in the rest of the world! How do you people survive if you're never allowed to sleep?'

27

Stunned and alert, Aama and Baba are perched on the edge of their seats as we zoom along the ring road around Paris in a zippy Ford C-Max. The expression on Aama's face tells us this is a fairly terrifying end to the longest day of her life.

Somehow, it's still 12 August and we've been on a rollercoaster of emotions since we arrived in France. There was pride when Aama burst out with her first French word, a hearty 'Bonjoo!' to the French immigration officer who checked her passport. Then there was fear and confusion as we entered the baggage hall and Aama crash-tackled Baba to the ground, saving him from drowning in a huge aquarium full of colourful fish. Then hysterical laughter when they discovered the aquarium was an optical illusion on the airport floor; a hologram projected from the ceiling to advertise some kind of pharmaceutical drug. There was awe and amazement when a moving, circular shelf made from black rubber delivered the suitcase Aama and Baba thought they'd lost forever when they handed it to a stranger in Kathmandu. This was followed by some tension between David and me when I insisted Baba was fine to go to the toilet unaccompanied because he's a grown man. Then complete and utter panic when I didn't see Baba take a wrong turn out of the bathroom and we lost him for eight and a half terrifying minutes … There was some justified anger when David barked that he'd told me so—and unimaginable relief when I found Baba at the other end of the airport, darting away from a French woman like a rugby player dodging a tackle. She had reached out to touch his arm when asking if he needed help and now he looked ready to run all the way back to Nepal, where people keep their hands to themselves.

Finally, came the moment of pure joy when Aama and Baba reunited with Véronique in the arrival hall of Paris Charles de Gaulle Airport. They hadn't been together for two years and now they ran to embrace one another, laughing and smiling and stroking each other's faces. Aama and Véronique have a deep, inexplicable connection and a shared vocabulary of just eight words. For some reason, they've never needed language to understand each other. In a world where verbal communication is considered a cornerstone of friendship, it defies all logic that our families have become so close when we can barely speak or understand each other. But it may even be *because* of this that we all choose to invest so much in these relationships. It's rare to experience something inexplicable and wondrous in the Information Age when it seems almost everything can be explained.

Now the five of us are driving towards David's sister's house, and Aama and Baba are far more petrified in the car than they were at any stage of the seven thousand kilometres they flew through the sky to get here.

They've been in plenty of cars before, but driving in the Himalayas comes with a few caveats. In Nepal, cars are almost always driven by men. The official speed limit on all Nepali roads, whether you're driving past a primary school or on a major highway, is 80 kph. However, it's rare to hit anywhere near that speed on their often narrow, winding roads which are full of potholes, traffic and wandering cows. Nepali people avoid travelling at night when sleepy drivers are more likely to slip off mountainous cliffs and plunge into a ravine. And although the Nepali government has outlined numerous road rules for their citizens, in my experience there are only two everyone seems to follow: just don't hit the car in front of you and toot your horn often so everyone knows you're coming. Oh, and stay on the left if you can manage it.

Now, we're hurtling down the autoroute on the *right-hand* side of the road, *not* blasting our horn, at *130 kph* in a car driven by a *woman,* and Aama is sitting bolt upright on the edge of her seat because she finally got what she wished for.

'Oh good,' Aama murmurs. '*Now* the sun decides to sleep. While we're driving ...'

It's ten in the evening and there's a sea of blinding white headlights snaking towards us on the other side of the road. On our side, hundreds of red taillights overtake us like missiles at 150 kph.

'It looks like we're driving down this side of the road with everyone else going in this direction,' Aama observes, 'and people going the other way are driving on the other side of the road.'

'Yep, that's the rule here,' says David.

'And everyone just does it?' Aama asks and David nods. 'What happens if they don't?'

'They'll probably crash and die,' David shrugs. 'But if they survive, the police will make them pay a huge fine and take their licence.'

'But how are they driving without tooting their horns?'

'Here, you only use it as a warning for danger. You don't actually need to toot your horn to drive a car.'

For reasons that aren't clear, this information tickles Baba and he laughs hysterically until we reach our destination.

28

We arrive at David's sister's empty house—a two-bedroom cottage in the south of Paris—and Véronique pushes open the front door. Inside, Aama spins in slow circles. Her mouth hangs open, her head rolling around to look at the ceiling and floors. She murmurs sounds of surprise and delight as she strokes the white painted walls and gleaming kitchen benchtops. Then she presses her nose against the decorative mirror and smiles at her tired reflection. When she sits on the grey couch, Aama sinks into the plush cushions and giggles as the furniture seems to gobble her up. She pokes the fabric and shakes her head in disbelief when her finger disappears into the sponge-like material.

'I've never seen furniture so soft! Is this your bed?'

'No, that's just a chair to sit on while you watch TV,' David explains, pointing to the flat screen, and Aama's eyes grow wide.

Minutes later, David's sister and her family arrive home and Aama and Baba leap to their feet for this momentous occasion. Aama has waited five years to meet the remaining four members of the French family she long ago adopted into her heart.

My sister-in-law, Catherine, is three years younger than David. So far the only thing I've found the siblings to have in common is their sense of humour and their ancestry. The first time I met Catherine at a dinner party in Paris, she told me her future plan was to buy a house, have children, *not* get married to her long-term boyfriend and keep building her already successful events management company. She was twenty-three years old at the time, with perfectly coiffed blond curls cascading onto her ironed shirt, and she knew exactly what she wanted from life. By comparison, her single, older brother was between jobs, wearing crinkled cheesecloth and still unsure if he would be in Australia or France next week. Or maybe Madagascar. Whatever. He'd work out a job when he got there.

Now Catherine is arriving home to her beautiful house (tick!) with her non-husband—a spirited and resourceful French-Russian named Greg (tick!)—and their two sweet, rambunctious children, Max and Hugo (tick!), after a holiday from her über-successful business (tick, tick, tick!). And now her brother and his wife—both unemployed and quite homeless on purpose—are standing in her living room with two elderly

Himalayan farmers.

Aama reaches out to Catherine, Greg, Max and Hugo one by one, cradling each of their faces and kissing both their cheeks with the tenderness of a mother reunited with her long-lost children. Standing a metre behind her, Baba grins and offers a respectful *namaste*. He's positioned and ready to bolt away from anyone who tries to kiss him, but the French sense his hesitancy and bring their palms together, mirroring his gesture with a smile.

Soon, Alain appears in the doorway and Aama marches up to the man who broke her heart a few weeks earlier in the village. Alain greets her warmly with a kiss on each cheek then Aama grabs both of his hands in her own and smiles up at him with compassion.

'I understand you now.' Aama fixes Alain's eyes while she pauses for me to translate. 'You only stayed one night in our house and I was very upset because I thought we did something wrong. But now I see it was just too hard for you. Now I've seen your sealed roads and fast cars, so I understand why it was too difficult to make the long journey to our house on foot. Our beds aren't as comfortable as the chair you sit on to watch TV,' Aama motions to the couch behind her. 'My house is small, so you hit your head when you come in the door because you are used to standing up straight in your kitchen. It was too hard for you, not because of our home, but because of where you come from. Look at this place!' Aama turns and gestures to the Parisian house around her.

It's only been an hour since she left the airport but Aama's already putting the pieces together, solving the puzzle of our family and our sometimes vexing, bewildering ways. She turns back to Alain and gives his hand a motherly pat.

'It's okay, brother. Now I understand you.'

29

When most people visit Paris for the first time, they head straight to the Eiffel Tower. But not Aama and Baba. They don't know what an Eiffel Tower is and we need to help them grasp some basics first. They're farmers, so they're more curious to find out where our food comes from and why our tea tastes so bloody awful. Compared to the rich dried tea leaves, spices and pepper that Aama grinds together with warm milk straight from the buffalo, English Breakfast tea with skim milk from a box tastes a bit like ox piss. At least that's what the expression on their faces indicates when David serves them a mug with a limp tea bag floating around in it. So, our first great French adventure is not to one of the most visited tourist icons on the planet, but to the good old *supermarché*.

The closest supermarket to Catherine's home happens to be one of the largest supermarkets in continental Europe. Regular supermarkets in Europe are bigger than most villages in Nepal, but this Carrefour is so huge the French call it a *hyper*market. Like a hyperactive supermarket. These megastores can be up to 23,000 square metres—which is bigger than every Bunnings Warehouse in Australia—and have a mind-exploding 80,000 *different* products for sale. The shelves contain everything from books to computers, toys and cosmetics, right down to fresh fish, haemorrhoid cream, blueberries, garden gnomes and bottles of wine.

I can't stand these places. The hospital lights, the plinkyplonky elevator music, the shameless marketing that convinces me I'll save money if I buy twelve of something when I really only need one. Every time I walk into a hypermarket, I end up buying the ingredients for an exotic meal I'll lose the will to cook as soon as I make it out of there alive. But Aama and Baba want to know where our food comes from and the supermarket is the only part of the food chain I actively engage with.

'This,' I open my arms and turn to face Aama and Baba, 'is where we get all our food!'

'Ehhh!' Aama breathes out as she walks through the doors, which swing open without her touching them before trapping her inside. She looks from the brightly coloured shampoo bottles on her left to a dozen television screens flickering with cartoon images on her right. Then she squints up at the fluorescent lights in the roof before bending down to touch the floor. 'It's cold,' she observes, running her hands over the smooth linoleum. I nod, as if I know this. It's never occurred to me to reach down and touch a supermarket floor before.

David pulls a shopping trolley from the parking bay and Aama and Baba approach it like I might approach a baby unicorn. They crouch down to examine the undercarriage of this magnificent silver basket, cooing as they run their hands over its cool, metal sides, and gently stroke the wheels. We push the cart through the hypermarket, past the sushi bar, the pharmacy counter and the dude in a bubble cutting people's hair for 10 euros. There's an actual fishmonger placing live crabs in giant aquariums and a full-service bakery with a bloke who looks like the Swedish chef from the Muppets, making fresh strawberry tarts. But the biggest surprise is in the fruit section where a tanned, muscly gentleman is doing some kind of salsa dancing by the pineapples. I can't be sure, but I think he's been employed to make the tropical fruit section feel more like a Caribbean market bazaar. It works, and I'm instantly overwhelmed with the desire to buy 8 kg of guava.

'There's more food in this room today than my family has grown in my entire life,' Aama exhales, pressing a hand to her chest to steady herself. She walks through the fresh produce section and admires the perfect shape of eight flawless tomatoes still joined together on a vine. There's a ginger root larger than Baba's hand, and fish the size of cats.

'This aubergine is bigger than my head!' Aama pokes out her tongue as she holds the deep purple fruit up to her cheek. 'How do they get it so shiny? None of our vegetables ever look like that.'

Later I will Google 'Why is supermarket produce so shiny?' and discover our fruit and vegetables are often covered in wax because urban consumers only want to eat pretty plants. But for now I just say, 'I don't know why, Aama, let me take a photo!'

Next, we turn into the supermarket aisle that completely rocks Aama's world.

The milk aisle.

In Australia, we tend to drink our milk fresh, so we buy cartons only as we need them and they live in the fridge. The French, however, consume long-life milk, which they buy in bulk and keep in the cupboard until it's opened. This is something I've always struggled to reconcile with their obsession with fresh food and reputation as gourmet connoisseurs.

In the village, milk is almost as valuable as water. Aama and Baba spend a huge chunk of their lives tending to their buffalo so that she produces two litres of milk for the family each day. Now they're standing between two walls of moo juice, their life source stacked from floor to ceiling in thousands of plastic bottles and cardboard boxes. I imagine they feel like I would if I was standing on a diving board above a swimming pool of cash, *à la* Scrooge McDuck.

'How long must it have taken to milk all these holy cows?' Aama places a reverent hand on a one-litre bottle of milk (worth 91 cents according to its price tag) and offers a blessing to the sacred dairy towers around her. Then she watches a shopper glide past us, talking on her mobile phone as she grabs a six-pack of milk cartons and tosses it into her trolley, with no thought or effort at all.

'No buffalo. No worries,' Aama muses, as the woman laughs into her telephone and strolls away. It took her less than three seconds to acquire what takes three days of hard, physical labour for Aama and Baba; and it comes shrink-wrapped and decorated with a picture of a cow wearing a top hat.

30

We arrive home to a house in full flight. It's past midday and the French are busy preparing for what I affectionately refer to as *le sport national.*

When I first married into David's family, one of the hardest things for me to adjust to was the amount of time they spend cooking and eating. I come from a 'food is fuel' and 'eat when you're hungry' kind of family, so it was a shock to find myself in a situation where it's more like 'food is love' and 'meals are an endurance test'. When our French family holiday together, it's not unusual to clock *ten hours* every day just on the preparation and consumption of food. Each morning, the family put (what seems like) the entire contents of their fridge and cupboards on the dining table for everyone to pick at over a long, lazy breakfast. Then as we pack everything away around mid-morning, the conversation turns to 'What's for lunch?' We've barely finished cleaning up from breakfast when someone starts cooking again. At 11.45 the cork comes out of the first bottle of wine for the day, we clink glasses for the *apéritif* and bang! We're sitting at the table again, eating our way through several courses—soup, salad, the main *plat,* then cheese and dessert. Then we clean up. Then we have a nap, because, you know, day-drinking. Then we wake up, ask 'What's for dinner?' and boom! We're back in the kitchen, cooking another nine-course meal. The sound of a champagne cork popping sometime between five and six calls everyone to the lounge room for another *apéritif* and some pre-dinner snacks. From there, you're destined to spend the rest of the evening at the table, staying much longer than you want or need to because you're so stuffed full of food you physically can't stand up.

For the French, I get the sense that mealtimes are where relationships are built and nurtured, where communication unfolds and stories are shared. They're a way for people to express love by serving each other meat drowned in butter and immaculately fluffed soufflés. Most important of all, they're a time to express opinions, argue about politics, unpack social issues and poke fun at each other until someone pretends to get offended. It's a whole thing. A bonding experience. At least in my French family. And in the beginning, when I couldn't speak a word of French, I enjoyed the whole process about as much as a Pap smear. Now that I speak French and can participate in the ritual, I love it for the important role it plays in our family life. I've now learnt to choose my clothes based on how 'fondue-friendly' they are. For me, even in Paris, fashion is not as important as being able to eat an entire baguette and a vat of melted Swiss cheese without losing blood circulation or undoing any buttons.

But *le sport national* is new to Aama and Baba so I'm conscious they might have a hard time adapting to mealtimes in Europe—particularly with the language barrier. Now we're all sitting at the table and Greg is rushing around the kitchen putting the finishing touches on today's main course: fresh barbecued trout he caught himself on a recent fishing trip.

'Greg is cooking our lunch today,' I smile and Aama's mouth drops open.

My brother-in-law works hard to be a self-sustainable member of society. Not only does he catch his own fish, but he plucks salad from the garden he planted in his backyard, cooks it all up for his family, does the dishes afterwards and feeds the scraps to his chickens. He's extremely hands-on at home, even by Western standards, and a man like this is about as common as Bigfoot in Nepal. So Aama can't take her eyes off him as he leaps around the open-plan kitchen, sautéing this, frying that and washing out the pans in the sink as he goes.

'It's like he knows everything!' Aama says. 'He *does* everything! He cooks, he cleans ...'

'Yep!' Catherine laughs and raises her glass, 'and I just sit around drinking wine!'

This isn't true, of course—she made half the food laid out on the table in front of us and works hard to pay for it all—but Aama's smile spreads so wide it has nowhere else to go.

The lunch passes in a flurry of food and language, conversations unfolding slowly as each sentence is translated between French, English, Nepali, Gurung and even a bit of Russian. When Aama and Baba finish the plates of food we serve them, they both look around the table, unsure what to do next. Aama is always the gatekeeper of food in her home. People only eat what she dishes out for them and she makes sure everyone is well fed before she'll consider eating anything herself. But here the food is just lying all over the table and no one seems to be in charge. It's chaos.

'If you're still hungry, you can help yourself to more food,' I tell them, and they look at me like I've suggested they strip naked and run around the block—kind of amused at the idea but also, no. That won't be happening.

'Honestly, it's okay,' David says, reaching for the salad servers and piling some rocket leaves onto his own plate to show them how it's done.

Aama looks sideways at Baba but he shakes his head vehemently, chuckles and says something to his wife in Gurung.

'Life is so different here ...' Aama hesitates before reaching for the tongs, torn between the discomfort of serving food she's had no hand in preparing, or letting her husband go hungry if she doesn't. Love wins and she grabs a piece of barbecued fish between the pincers, then looks up at us, checking all our faces for any indication that she has misunderstood. When we smile and nod, encouraging her to continue, Aama winces like she's having a tooth pulled and drops the fish on Baba's plate.

31

Round Three of *le sport national* finishes at around nine, but the sun is still shining and Aama becomes distressed. It's now been twenty-four hours since they arrived in this strange new world and they're jetlagged and 'over' everything—overwhelmed, overstimulated and definitely overfed. It's not unusual for them to be asleep at nine in Nepal, but as long as there is light left in the day, they refuse to go to bed.

'We could play Just Dance on the Nintendo Wii!' Max suggests to the table of flagging adults, all propping our heads up with our hands.

Video games?

'Nope. No way,' I shake my head.

'Why not?!' everyone says. 'It'll be fun! What's the problem?'

I know Aama and Baba will be exposed to it at some point on this trip, but *I'm* not ready. I don't know how to explain to them that we have so much money and free time in our society that we can afford to spend both on jumping around in front of the television after dinner. That we follow the dance moves of a computer-programmed silhouette to score imaginary points that don't mean anything while farmers back in the village are working for seventeen hours a day just to grow the same amount of food we ate as a pre-dinner snack. A wave of crippling shame washes over me and I tell the family the Nintendo just feels like too much. Too soon. But they tell me I'm overreacting and I'm quickly overruled.

Later that night we upload images of Baba dancing on Facebook. He's gripping the Wii in his hand and mimicking the electronic dancer on the screen with surprising energy and precision. His grandchildren in Nepal respond in shock, because in his almost eight decades on the planet, no one in his family has seen him dance before. Not even Aama. With his *topi* perched on his head, our seventy-eight-year-old Baba follows the little blue dancer on the screen for three breathless minutes, arms flailing, grinning through the entire performance, and beats David in a landslide. Aama is up next, giggling as she takes on Catherine in an epic Bollywood battle. When the song ends, she flops down next to me with an exhausted, exhilarated laugh.

'You see? No buffalo, no worries!' she says for the second time that day.

'What do you mean by that, Aama?' I ask.

'Well, if I want my family to stay healthy and strong, I need milk. And if I want milk, I need a buffalo. But buffaloes are expensive and when you get one, you have to work hard to take care of her. Every single day you cut her grass and milk her. You clean her stable. You take her into the fields. In the village, there are no days off from taking care of a buffalo. But here, you can do lots of work in one day to earn enough money to buy milk for weeks. Then you can just pour it from a bottle when you need it and take a whole day off to dance in front of your TV. You people have a *good life,*' she emphasises, as night falls and she rises to go to bed.

'No buffalo, no worries.'

32

When I took a friend of mine to see the Eiffel Tower for the first time, I was shocked to find her unimpressed.

'Hmm. It's just a giant lump of twisted metal, isn't it?'

I was almost insulted. Seeing this iconic tower used to be one of my wildest, giddiest dreams and I *still* get a rush of excitement every time I see it. Objectively, I guess the wrought-iron lattice monument may not be the most beautiful thing in France, but it's certainly the most recognisable. It was originally designed as the entrance arch to the World Fair held in 1889, and at 300 metres tall it was the fanciest damn doorway the world had ever seen. This incredible feat of engineering was only supposed to be a temporary fixture but, even so, the people of Paris came together to protest against the construction of what they considered a 'useless and monstrous' structure. They claimed it looked like a giant black smokestack, a pimple on the face of Paris. But the tower was built anyway and has been there ever since. Whoever was tasked with tearing it down must have thought it might be useful one day, and they were right. The Eiffel Tower and France have become mutually symbolic, as if one can't exist without the other. The hideous doorway is now the most recognised tourist monument in the world, injecting 60 million euros into the French economy each year from the 25,000 people who visit *every single day*. These people aren't flocking to the Eiffel Tower because it looks like a giant pimple. For many first-time visitors to Paris, this pointy lump of twisted metal is symbolic of something greater. Romance. Magic. A long-held dream coming true …

Aama and Baba have never heard of the Eiffel Tower. It's the tallest structure they've ever seen so they marvel at its size for a few minutes, but don't display any of the wonder they showed when they saw Catherine's soft couch or the beautiful no smoking signs on the plane.

'What does it do?' Aama asks.

'It's a tourist attraction,' I explain. 'It used to be the doorway for a big festival but now people go up the top so they can see the whole city.'

'It's not a factory or a brick kiln?' Aama scrunches up her face. 'Why would they go to the trouble of building something this big if it's not used to make something?'

I look up and see how Aama, like the former residents of Paris, might also think it resembles an industrial smokestack. But what she's really asking is, 'What's the point of your big, fancy tower if it doesn't do anything?'

'I think they might use it for our communication network,' I guess (correctly as it turns out), and Aama murmurs and nods her approval. Then a street performer dressed like a fluorescent green ancient Egyptian pharaoh skips up to our group and asks us for money. They greet him with shock, surprise and wondrous enthusiasm, and the giant telecommunication tower behind them is forgotten.

We soon discover most of the normal tourist hotspots hold little interest for Aama and Baba.

The Champs-Élysées? 'It's a nice street.'

The glass pyramid at the Louvre. 'Hmm. That's a lot of windows.'

The miniature version of the Statue of Liberty. 'What's a New York?'

However, there are two things Aama and Baba find truly fascinating in Paris. Firstly, they can't believe the 'skinny, delicious potato things' served with lunch are made from the same spuds that grow in their garden. It's love at first crunch and the beginning of a devoted month-long relationship between Aama, Baba and the humble French fry.

Secondly, they're curious about our holy sites like the Sacré-Cœur Basilica, Notre Dame and other churches around the city. Or, to be more specific, the macabre artwork depicting a well-known carpenter painted on their walls.

33

Aama once described herself to me as an 'uneducated' Buddhist. She identifies as a Buddhist and performs many Buddhist rituals but, like many Gurung people, her personal spiritual practice borrows heavily from Nepal's more prominent religion, Hinduism. When preparing for this trip, we asked Aama if she wanted to bring her devotional equipment, like her incense and *ting-sha* cymbals, so she could continue her morning and evening *puja*.

'No, it's not necessary. Everything I need for my religious practice I carry in here,' Aama patted her chest.

Nevertheless, I can see a sense of relief and peace wash over Aama as we step inside the churches of Paris. She seems immediately at home in our places of worship, even though they bear no resemblance to her temples in Nepal. We drop some coins in the box at the doorway and take four candles, which Aama and Baba light with great reverence. Then they place them on the candelabra along with a dozen other flickering prayers, before taking a few moments to add their own.

I guide them towards the pews so they can take a moment to pause and reflect on their surroundings and, as we enter, a security guard hisses at Baba to remove his hat. I whisper a translation to Aama and she spins around to Baba and screams into his good ear in Gurung.

'Take off your *topi!*'

Everyone in the church whips their head around to locate the source of this unknown language reverberating off the walls. I place a finger over my lips, signalling for Aama and Baba to be quiet, but it seems that gesture doesn't mean the same thing where they're from.

'Who's that guy?' Aama asks in a loud voice, raising her chin and pointing her lips at the image of a man on the wall.

'Jesus Christ,' I whisper, hoping it will catch on.

Aama lowers her voice slightly, 'Well, what's he doing up there?'

I want to say he's nailed to the cross, but my Nepali

vocabulary doesn't quite stretch that far.

'He's dead,' is all I can manage.

'Dead?' Aama bellows, as she looks back to poor Jesus.

Throughout the church, dozens of people who were trying to pray in peace are now giving us the evil eye. I flash them an apologetic smile, grateful they can't understand how this train wreck of a conversation is unfolding.

'Almost dead, maybe.' I correct myself. On second thoughts, I have no idea if he's *post-crucifixion* in these images, or if the grisly event is still underway.

Aama screws up her face and gestures in his direction. 'But why?'

Does she mean why is he dying? Or why is there a dead man hanging on the wall of a holy place? Unfortunately, I don't have an answer for either of those questions.

I should, though, because technically, I'm kind of a Catholic. I was born and christened as a Catholic and I went through the whole process of Reconciliation and Communion. My family was kicked out of the church before my Confirmation because of a dispute with our priest regarding the holiness of our family dog. That was the end of my religious career and I haven't picked up a bible since I was eight. So, I'm definitely not the best person to explain Christianity in Nepali or any language. I can't recall why Jesus was crucified and I should just say 'I don't know', but a line from Monty Python pops into my head and gives me the false confidence to wing it.

He's not the Messiah, he's a very naughty boy!

'Christian people believe there is only one god,' I continue in my caveman Nepali, pointing to the man who is dead or dying on the cross. 'Jesus Christ is the son of God. Or is a man who is made like God. Something like that. He is a carpenter. He makes bread into fish and water into wine, so he has a lot of friends. Some people think he's God. Other people think he's not God. They think he's a bad man. So they killed him. But later he woke up.'

Aama nods along as I speak, her eyes fixed on Jesus. Hindus worship 330 million mostly-unnamed deities—some of which are axe-wielding elephants or blue humans with eight arms and legs—so this may all sound plausible so far.

'But why is he *naked?*'

I look back at Jesus and the flimsy piece of cloth draped around his hips. 'That's a very good question, Aama.'

We both stare up at the cross for a minute or two in silence before Aama quizzes me again.

'Where is he from?'

'He was born in Bethlehem,' I say. For a moment I feel smug that I know the answer to one of her questions, but then I remember he was Jesus of *Nazareth*. And doesn't Jerusalem have something to do with all of this?

'Where is this place?'

'Palestine, I think. Some might say Israel. It's complicated. People are still fighting about it. There's a big war. It's near Saudi Arabia. You know the place with all the sand you saw from the plane?'

'*God* lives in that sandy place?'

'No, not God. Just his son. This guy,' I point my lips towards

Jesus.

'Do a lot of people believe this?' Aama asks, and when I nod she presses further. 'Do you believe this?'

'No,' I shake my head. 'I believe Jesus lived and he was a good man, but I'm not sure about the other stuff.'

'Is it hot where he's from?'

That's a random question.

'Maybe,' I shrug. 'In the summer, for sure.'

'That's probably why he's naked.' Aama nods, satisfied with that explanation.

'Could be.'

'So they killed him and he came back from the dead? Then what happened?'

I have no fricking idea.

'Um, everyone was very happy,' I guess, 'and now we have a holiday every year to celebrate.'

'What kind of holiday?'

'Well, our family comes together for lunch and an enormous bunny rabbit comes to the house to deliver colourful eggs and chocolates to the children.'

'That's nice,' Aama nods, somehow accepting *that* explanation without question. 'And who are those people in the sky?'

I hold up a finger for Aama to wait as I flip through the dictionary and find the translation.

'*Svargadūtalē*' I sound it out and Aama looks at me, her expression blank. I say the word four more times, rearranging the emphasis on different syllables each time in case it makes a difference.

It does not. And we're off for Round Two...

'They're flying people.'

'These people can fly?' Aama wriggles in her seat and sits upright again. 'Are these real, live humans?'

'Um, no. They're...' If I couldn't translate 'tuna fish sandwich with fries' at lunchtime, what hope do I have explaining the role of benevolent celestial beings who act as intermediaries between God and humanity?

'They're dead too?' Aama recoils and I fumble though the dictionary, desperate to find better words.

'No, no, not dead. But not alive. Something in between. They're good people!' I smile and hold up my thumbs, nodding enthusiastically. 'They wear white clothes. They have wings like birds. They're God's friends. They fly around and help people.'

Angels, for crying out loud. Freaking ANGELS.

We both go quiet for a moment and look up at Jesus and his mates. The look on Aama's face is a mixture of confusion and repulsion. She's used to going to temples where Buddha sits cross-legged on a lotus looking peaceful and enlightened. Now, somehow I've painted the Catholic Church to look a bit like a zombie apocalypse with colourful sweets and magic rabbits. I shake my head, utterly ashamed of how this whole conversation has gone down and I make a silent apology in my head to my dear Christian friends. I make a mental note to attempt this explanation again at the end of the trip when I hope my Nepali has improved, I've brushed up on the Israeli-Palestinian conflict and Googled 'Christianity for Dummies'. Then, after a few moments of reflection, I send a quick apology skyward to God. You know, just in case. Then I look back at Aama.

'Do you want to go?' I whisper.

'Yes, I do.' She's already on her feet and we bolt for the door.

34

Martine and Philippe are like an aunt and uncle for David. They're curious to get to know these famous Nepalese farmers they've heard so much about, so after our day out in Paris, we drop by their house for the *apéritif*. Alain has warned them that the only way to get Baba talking is to hand him a drink, so as soon as we arrive, Philippe cracks open an enormous treasure chest full of booze and tells Baba to take his pick. Then, when everyone's glasses are filled, Martine and Philippe start asking questions.

'Philippe is asking what your home and village is like?' I translate. 'He wants to know how life is different in Nepal?'

'Our life is difficult,' Aama's voice is hard. 'Our houses are small and old. Our roads are terrible. Our beds are uncomfortable.' She looks like she's in pain, spitting out every word. 'My village is not good. My *country* is not good.'

'That is not true, Aama,' I gasp, pressing a hand into my stomach where it feels like the wind has been knocked out of me. 'Your home and country are beautiful.'

Aama is the proudest Nepali woman I know. The love she has for her village radiates through everything she does, from the care she takes when sweeping her kitchen floor to her passion and confidence when she's addressing her community as their leader and chief. But now her face is creased with sadness and confusion, as if everything she thought she knew about her life has been thrown into question.

At this point you might think: 'Well, duh! What did you think was going to happen when you take someone from one of the poorest countries in the world and drop them in one of the richest?' And you're right. We expected this. We prepared for it. I'd imagined hundreds of scenarios and planned how I would respond. But now my brain has gone blank.

'It's so clean here,' Baba croaks, smacking the rum between his lips. 'There's no rubbish on the ground.'

'Europe is good!' Aama says with an authoritative nod and two thumbs up in the air. 'Nepal is not good. We are poor. We have nothing.'

'Nepal is a wonderful country with good people,' I push back, while David translates in the background so his family can follow the conversation.

'Why do you think we come back to your village and your family every year? You should be proud of your home. You've built it with your own hands. You have mountains and clean air and healthy food growing in your fields.'

'Yes, but you have skinny, delicious potato things and milk that comes from a bottle,' Aama argues.

'But we have no idea where those things come from, Aama,

or what chemicals have been put in them. At least you know your potatoes are natural and your milk is fresh,' I counter. 'Remember what you said to me this morning when we were walking through Paris? You said you never knew there were so many different kinds of beautiful. Remember?'

Aama tilts her head slightly to the side, a half-hearted Nepali gesture of agreement. Before we set out on this journey I had shared with Aama my travelling motto: *It's not right, it's not wrong, it's just different.* This is the mantra I was taught to chant when, at sixteen years young, I spent a year in Norway as an AFS exchange student and 'ambassador for peace'.

'There is no better and no worse,' I insist. 'There is no good and no bad. Like you said, there are just *many different kinds of beautiful.*'

'Ehhh, it's true. Your rice tastes like plastic. Your toilets are ridiculous. And this tea you drink from a bag—' Aama's face contorts in disgust and we all laugh. 'But I guess these things could be beautiful, too.'

The conversation then pivots towards food, and I hope that's the end of any more anti-Nepal talk. Back in the village, Aama always asked such intelligent questions about how we do things in Australia and Europe that she helped me see my culture as it looks from the outside—the good, the bad and the utterly absurd. Setting out on this adventure, the thing I most looked forward to was being able to explore the 'normal' in our culture through Aama's discerning eyes. Her perspective is often insightful, while also being so obvious that I don't know why I never drew the same conclusion myself. But now that she's here, she can no longer look at our society objectively because she's blinded by clean streets, comfy mattresses, coffee machines and fast cars. All she sees now is how hard her life seems compared to ours. A fact that is as unsurprising as it is true.

35

When Aama and Baba wake up the next morning, something's off.

They smile when they walk into the lounge room and see us all sitting around the breakfast table, but their eyes are weary and sad. They take their seats just as Catherine bursts through the front door gripping an enormous bag of hot croissants.

'Good morning!' Catherine sings. 'Here's breakfast!'

They barely acknowledge her but I flash a warm smile at my sister-in-law. I realise she's suffering from the same affliction that's plagued me for the last five years.

I call it 'My Husband is a God' syndrome.

The Western man seems like a superior being because he does men's *and* 'women's' work. I could do a triple backflip over this breakfast table and it would be just as awe-inspiring for Aama as when David singlehandedly makes her a cup of tea.

Yesterday, Aama and Baba showered praise on Greg for bringing these delicious crescent moons of flaky butter from the bakery, and Catherine is probably hoping to get the same reaction today. She doesn't. But I don't think their lack of enthusiasm has anything to do with Catherine or her croissants.

'Is everything okay?' I ask Aama for the third time this morning. 'Did you have a bad sleep?'

'Everything's fine,' Aama pulls at her croissant, smothers it in jam and pushes it into her mouth. 'Good sleep,' she assures me with a tilt of her head. The table goes silent again.

They've seemed quiet ever since we left Martine and Philippe's last night.

'Okay!' I say, clasping my hands together like a kindergarten teacher and smiling at Aama and Baba with way too much enthusiasm. 'Today we'll pack all our clothes and drive two hours north to Véronique's house in Normandy. When we arrive, we can go see the ocean!'

'*Samundra?*' Aama's lips curl upward just slightly. Nepal is a landlocked country and Aama has only ever seen the ocean in pictures.

'Yes! Today we'll go to the beach, then we'll stay with Véronique for most of the week. Is that okay?'

Aama looks at Baba, who is staring straight ahead, then she starts yelling into his good ear in Gurung. He croaks a few words at Aama and she fires a tirade of language back at him in anger. They exchange a verbal gunfight in Gurung, which we can't understand, then they fall silent. Baba looks down at his hands and Aama turns to us and forces a smile.

'How many days is it since we left Kathmandu?' Aama raises her chin towards us.

'Four days,' I hold up four fingers for Baba to see.

'Four days!' Aama yells into Baba's ear.

'Four days?' Baba strains.

'Yes!'

Baba says something to Aama in Gurung and she turns back to us, her eyes downcast.

'Four days feels like a long time, doesn't it? If we stay one month …'

Her voice trails off and David and I look at each other in horror. *Ah crap, they want to go home.*

'You don't want to stay for the whole month?' I ask, the rising pitch of my voice doing nothing to hide my internal panic.

'I don't know,' Aama fidgets in her chair. 'We have no money to give you for all of this. And we don't even know how much you're spending because you pay for everything with that little piece of plastic.'

'But you're our guests. It's like when we're guests in *your* home and you do everything for us. We don't pay you anything.'

'But what are we going to do for a month? We're not working. We just eat and sleep and look at things. We visit places. We don't do anything *productive*,' Aama argues.

'That's because you're on holiday, Aama,' David says. 'Do you know what a holiday is?'

Aama swipes a playful hand at David. 'How would I know what a holiday is? I've never had a holiday in my life!'

'Well, when we're on holiday, we don't work,' I explain. 'We visit new places. We eat. We spend time with our family. We try new things. We *relax*. That's a holiday.'

'In France, it's compulsory,' David points out. 'Everyone has to take five weeks holiday away from their job every year.'

'But I don't understand *why*,' Aama says.

Is it because we're lazy and self-indulgent? Or does it go deeper than that? Why are holidays so important in our culture that even our governments have enshrined the practice in law? I chew on my bottom lip, trying to come up with an answer that will satisfy not just Aama, but me, too.

Well, obviously, holidays are fun. And relaxing. When we get out of our routine and explore new places, we see the world from a new perspective. Sometimes we might even change our habits or way of thinking. But sometimes we just need a break from work and life. To rest and recharge. Because life can be stressful sometimes and stress is bad for our … aha!

'In our culture, we believe that holidays are good for your *health*.'

'Ehh,' Aama brightens, 'taking a holiday brings you good health?'

'Yes!' David and I exclaim in unison.

'Health is important,' Aama agrees. 'If we're sick we can't work, and if we can't work we can't eat. We can't do anything if we have poor health.'

'Exactly,' David and I exhale.

'We believe that if you don't make time for your health now, you'll need to make time for being sick later. So maybe we can try the holiday thing a bit longer?' I venture, 'and if you've had enough by the end of the week, I promise we'll book you on the next flight home.'

I sit back in my chair while I watch Aama translate all of

this to Baba. There's an emotion gurgling inside me that I'm struggling to identify. Guilt, perhaps? Shame that I've spent most of my adult life raging against the nine-to-five, determined to find an alternative to the capitalist system of 'working till I die'? As if I, with all my weekend getaways and annual leave entitlements, have any idea what that actually means.

36

We take the scenic route to Normandy, pulling off the autoroute onto winding country roads where we pass a pick-your-own open-air 'supermarket'—a communal farm where you pluck your own fruit and vegetables straight from Mother Earth. David slams on the brakes and chucks a U-turn into the driveway. He thinks Aama and Baba might feel better if they can connect with their 'inner farmer', and I'm willing to try anything at this point.

Here, instead of a trolley near the cash registers you grab a wheelbarrow from the barn. If you want to fully embrace the faux farmer experience you can even borrow gumboots. I didn't even know these places existed until today, but it's not a well-kept secret. There are dozens of families here, harvesting their produce fresh from the trees while literally frolicking through the fields in the summer sunshine.

When you live off the land, there's a rhythm and routine

you follow in order to survive. Now on holiday, this lifelong cycle has been disrupted for Aama and Baba, so it makes sense they're feeling lost and insecure. It's a Band-Aid fix, but we roll up our trousers and go clomping through the mud, hoping close proximity to the familiar process of growing and harvesting food might restore some temporary balance to their world.

When we enter a greenhouse full of heirloom tomatoes, hanging from the vine like thousands of bumpy Christmas baubles, Aama and Baba's expressions look like mine when I find a crumpled $20 note in the pocket of an old pair of jeans.

'It's not *possible!*' Aama squeals, following the enormous vine to the Roma tomatoes, then the cherry tomatoes and finally the red beefsteak tomatoes she's been trying so hard to grow in the village.

'Forget what I said about going back to Nepal,' Aama stops and holds up her palms. 'I've changed my mind. I want to live in this great white tomato tent forever.'

Over the next hour, we pluck plums direct from the trees, pick a kilo of capsicums we don't need and wander through a field of sunflowers. Then we hop back in the car, Aama and Baba's spirits restored, and continue our journey towards the Normandy coastline.

It's low tide when we arrive so the beach looks like a great sandy desert with a glittering, distant mirage. There are several hundred metres of sand between us and the water's edge and the beach stretches for a kilometre to the east and west either side. Even though we can barely see the water sparkling on the horizon, Aama is terrified to step off the paved esplanade onto the sand.

'I can't swim,' Aama panics. 'What if the water rushes back towards us?'

'Don't worry, Aama, it's miles away,' I say. 'It will come up here later, but slowly. Slower than you can walk. Then it will go back out again.'

'But how?'

'Because of the moon,' I smile and step out onto the sand. I dance a little jig to show her it's safe.

Aama moves towards the edge of the footpath and hesitates. I put out a hand to help her but she frowns and brushes me away. With her eyes fixed on the horizon, she sucks in a breath for courage and steps out alone. Her tiny feet drop onto the sand and she alternates her weight between them for a moment, assessing how to keep herself balanced on trillions of movable grains. Then she begins striding towards the water, stumbling on the soft sand, her eyes never leaving the ocean. Baba follows, his mouth twisted into a permanent grin as he staggers across the uneven ground, trying to keep pace with his wife.

'*Samundra,*' Aama breathes out when we step from dry sand to moist, approaching the water's edge. A gentle wave of sparkling blue diamonds laps the shore.

Aama giggles. Then she laughs and closes her eyes to feel the warmth of the sun. It's beaming down from the sky and reflecting up from the shallow puddles all around us. In the wet sand, Aama and Baba's shoes start to sink. Panicked, they kick them off before the beach swallows them whole. Now an uncertain grin spreads across their faces as they wriggle their toes in the gooey, gritty grains beneath their feet.

We spend half an hour just watching the ocean. Aama picks up shells and rubs them between her fingers and Baba hovers around some local kids collecting clams in a plastic bucket. Looking back to the dry sand, Aama notices a raucous group of teenagers playing badminton and some people—mostly women—lying on towels in bikinis. Some of them are reading books.

Aama points her lips towards them, 'What are these people doing?'

'They're on holiday, like you,' I grin. 'So they're resting, playing games, reading books.'

'They're not wearing a lot of clothes,' Aama observes, looking around for more pieces to the puzzle. 'Like the dying man in the temple yesterday. And this place is sandy too, isn't it? But it's not *hot* here ...' The cogs are turning.

It's a balmy sixteen degrees in the Normandy summer and it seems Aama's entire theory for why Jesus was half-naked on the cross has fallen apart.

'No, these people are wearing bikinis not because it's hot, but because it's *sunny*,' I explain. 'In Europe, many people lie in the sun because they want their skin to go darker.'

Aama spins around and glares at me.

'Are you making a joke?'

I shake my head. 'Many white people believe they'll be more beautiful if their skin is darker. They even use creams on their body that make them look more brown.'

'But in Nepal everyone is brown and wants to be more

white,' Aama stammers. 'We believe the *lighter* your skin, the more beautiful you look. How can you think dark is beautiful?'

A person's skin colour provides a visible marker of their social status in Nepal. Labourers and farmers are recognisable as working class because their skin is darkened from long days toiling in the sun. Anyone rich enough to buy their food instead of growing it spends more time inside where their skin is protected from the elements. They can also afford to buy beauty products that chemically lighten their skin—a billion-dollar industry in Asia where people bleach themselves beautiful. Therefore, the maths in Nepal is simple: light skin equals wealth; dark skin equals poverty. So why on earth would a rich person want to lie around in the sun trying to make themselves look poor?

I don't know how to explain to Aama that many white Europeans want to *appear* browner because they believe it looks better, but they won't face any of the social challenges or prejudice that come with being a person of colour. We can bake in the sun and use spray tans to darken our complexion but still reap all the benefits of white privilege. At the same time, people of colour in our society continue to battle against systemic racism that oppresses and discriminates against them *because* they have darker skin. It's all messed up. But I barely have the vocabulary to address or unpack these injustices in my own language and I'm worried that if I try, it'll turn into another 'holy dead guy and the magic rabbits' conversation. So, I keep it simple.

'In Europe, if you look pale like me, people might think I

look sick. When I go on holiday and get a tan, people tell me I look healthy.'

'This is crazy,' Aama shakes her head and laughs. 'You think browner is beautiful, and we think whiter is beautiful. So, what is beautiful? And who gets to decide?'

37

'I think I get it now!' Aama declares as she emerges from her bedroom one morning. 'I *am* working every day in France. It's just that my work here is to eat, sleep and look at stuff. I am an explorer. That's my job now.'

This positive reframe gives the journey and its struggles some purpose and Aama and Baba decide to stay in Europe for the entire month. Well, at least Aama decides to stay, and Baba won't leave without her.

The first week is an enormous adjustment for all of us. Just like us in the village, Aama and Baba now find themselves having to relearn basic life skills they thought they'd mastered decades ago, like eating, washing and going to the toilet. After spending a combined 141 years eating rice and lentils with their hands for almost every meal, they're overwhelmed by the huge variety of food in France and how to get it from their plate to their mouths with tiny silver weapons. Just as I often finish dinner in Nepal looking like I've been in a food fight, Aama and Baba's attempts at using cutlery sometimes send entire meals catapulting across the room. They've never used a knife and fork before, or eaten from flat, glossy plates. In the West, we learn this at such a young age that we don't realise what an impressive skill we've mastered, or the precision required to apply just the right amount of pressure to cut food into tiny morsels. If Aama or Baba press a fraction too hard on their knife or fork, the cutlery slips across the polished ceramic and knocks everything in its path onto the floor or someone's lap.

As if eating is not stressful enough, there's also the issue of Baba's teeth. Or rather, his abundance of gums. When he's deciding what to have for lunch, he doesn't seem to factor in his ability to chew it. I'm spending every meal with one eye on Baba while half sitting on my chair, poised and ready to jump up to administer the Heimlich manoeuvre (which I've now Googled and practised on David a few times, just in case).

Another thing we hadn't considered is that in the village, life happens at ground level. When we first arrived in Nepal, David and I both struggled with back pain from always sitting cross-legged to eat and cook on the mud-packed kitchen floor. Now, Aama is suffering from back pain from sitting on our ultra 'comfortable', cushion-covered chairs. Sometimes, mid-meal, she can't bear the pain anymore and either slides herself down to the floor or pulls her legs up to relieve the pressure on muscles we don't even know we're using when we sit.

Then there's the issue of showering.

In Sundara, villagers 'shower' about once a week—even though they spend all day, every day, working their fields doing some seriously sweaty stuff in subtropical heat. This may seem shocking for people in our society but there are plenty of scientific studies to suggest washing ourselves daily is unnecessary. In fact, many dermatologists argue that showering every day is *bad* for our skin because it strips us of our natural oils and good bacteria.

In the village, I only shower every three days or so. It doesn't matter because the smoke from the kitchen fire annihilates our sense of smell and masks any stench. When no one around us uses any beauty products, we all smell more or less the same anyway. It only becomes a problem when we wash our hair with hibiscus shampoo and scrub our bodies with frangipani body wash, removing our skin's natural oils before replacing them with a coconut-infused moisturising cream. Then, if we stand next to someone who smells like an actual human being, they seem dirty to us because *we* smell like a Caribbean cocktail.

This is the issue we face when, after a week of travelling together, Aama and Baba still haven't washed. Every morning we ask if they want a shower, and every morning they say no, so we stop asking. Then on day eight, Aama raises her chin towards the bathroom and says, 'Maybe today?'

I launch into Shower 101 before she changes her mind, being careful to explain everything in explicit detail, even if it seems obvious.

'First, you take off all your clothes.'

'Everything?' Aama's eyes widen.

'Everything,' I nod. 'The door will be shut so no one can see you.'

I show her a silver handle fixed to the shower wall and demonstrate how she can turn it right to make cold water come out of a disc suspended from the ceiling. Then I turn it all the way left and let the hot water run until it's scalding so that she understands how badly she could burn herself. Before leaving, I set the water to warm and explain which products are designed for which body parts and how to use them.

'Any questions?' Aama shakes her head as I back towards the door. 'Remember, it's hot! Don't burn yourself. Careful not to slip! I'm right outside the door if you need me.'

I pull up a chair and sit with my back against the bathroom door like a crazy person. I'm imagining all the things that could go wrong when a sixty-three-year-old woman strips naked and has the first hot shower of her life, alone in a tiled room rather than in an exposed courtyard surrounded by her neighbours.

When the door flings open 15 minutes later, Aama floats out of the bathroom shrouded in steam. A dopy smile hangs from her rosy cheeks. Her eyes are sparkling as she gently squeezes the water from her hair. She looks completely stoned.

'How was that, Aama?'

Aama reaches up, places two strong hands on each of my shoulders and stares into my eyes, dazed.

'You people are gods,' she says, her voice low and serious. 'How could you create a hot waterfall inside your house if you are not a god? As long as I live, I will never forget this day.'

She towel-dries her hair, wringing the last remnants of the shower from her fine, wispy braid. Then she drops her towel to the side and looks up at me.

'I'm so sorry, Laura Maya,' Aama bows her head and places a solemn hand across her chest. 'All these years you've returned to stay in my home, even though you could never have a shower there. Now I understand what a sacrifice you've made. Thank you for always coming back to stay with us anyway.'

'Are you kidding, Aama?' I laugh, putting an arm around her shoulders and giving her an affectionate squeeze. 'Nothing beats a bucket of cold water over the head after a hot day working in the village. Just different kinds of beautiful, right?'

38

Aama and Baba's first week in Europe can be summarised with one simple phrase: *chakai pariyo*.

The first time we heard Aama say it was in the milk aisle at the supermarket, and both she and Baba have said it hundreds of times since. We can't find a translation in the dictionary or on Google, but we know *chakai pariyo* is the metal box in the kitchen with the light inside that cooks your food by spinning it around in a circle and beeping when it's done. *Chakai pariyo* is also the even bigger box near the sink that magically transforms dirty plates, cutlery and glasses into clean ones overnight.

Chakai pariyo is the taste of fresh strawberries and ice cream. It's also the miniature cars that adults put their babies in so they don't have to carry them around on their backs. Even more, *chakai pariyo* is when people are pushing these prams along the beach esplanade but instead of a baby, there's a *chihuahua* inside. Because compared to the animals they're used to seeing, a chihuahua looks much more like a rat than a dog, and there would be no reason to parade either around in public in a tiny carriage like a king.

We call one of Aama's children to ask what *chakai pariyo* means and they tell us it's a Nepali expression of intense shock and surprise. It's a powerful phrase, yet somehow it fails to encapsulate the emotion Aama and Baba feel one night when we almost *chakai pariyo* both of them into cardiac arrest.

That night, we're heading out to a festival on the beach, but when we leave the house a noise catches Aama's attention.

'What's that, Laura Maya?' Aama gravitates towards the loud engine noise, and I follow her to the gate to get a better look. In front of the neighbour's house, there's a man chugging up and down a tiny strip of grass on a ride-on lawnmower.

'He's cutting the grass.'

'No, that's not possible …'

When Aama's family heads out to the fields every day to cut grass for the buffalo, their only tool is a curved machete. If there's not enough grass on the ground, they have to go up, climbing into the trees to source foliage as an alternative. When they manage to fill a large basket with grass and leaves, they carry the heavy load on their backs through the terraced fields to the buffalo stable.

Yet if this man is indeed cutting grass as we suggest, somehow he's doing it while sitting on a motorised buggy, smoking a cigarette.

Aama calls Baba over and they both stand dumbstruck, their hands gripping the top of the gate as they watch the man do laps of the lawn.

'Is he really cutting grass with a car?' Baba croaks.

'Where does the grass go?' Aama asks.

'It collects in a box underneath,' David explains.

'And then he feeds it to his buffalo?'

'No, I don't think he has a buffalo. He probably just throws it away.'

Aama and Baba glare up at David.

'What a waste! Do you know how long it would take us to cut that much grass?' Aama cries. 'Why does he bother?'

'So it, um … looks pretty?' David stammers, shooting me a desperate look over their heads.

'You don't need humans in your world,' Aama remarks. 'You've built machines that replace humans for everything. That's why you need so much money—because you buy the machines that do all the work for you. To earn money you have to work in jobs that take you out of your home so you can't raise your own children. You work to pay for a machine to cut your grass, but we cut our grass by hand. For free. You wouldn't need to work so much or earn all that money if you did more things with your bodies. Like we do.'

We all fall silent. These truths linger in the air alongside the scent of petrol and freshly mowed grass.

'That's probably why the people in your country are so fat,' Aama concludes. 'Your machines work harder than your bodies. Even your cows are fat.'

In case we haven't understood, Aama emphasises her point by holding her elbows out to the side, clenching her fists and puffing up her cheeks so she looks like a sumo wrestler preparing for battle. Unfortunately, the heavy-set gentleman riding the lawnmower chooses that exact moment to look up. Not only does he find he has an audience, but there's a tiny foreign lady across the street making an obvious gesture about his weight. He turns pink with rage.

David and I exchange a panicked glance and usher Aama and Baba back towards the car, then Véronique sweeps in behind us and flashes an award-winning smile at her furious neighbour.

'They're from Nepal!' she sings over the fence. 'They've never seen such a *huge lawnmower* before. Very big. Very wide lawnmower. They're very impressed!'

39

Over the ocean, the sun is slipping below the horizon as a large crowd gathers on the beach. Hawkers wander among the hundreds of people milling around on the sand, selling fairy floss and glow sticks. A cold wind whips around us and we help Aama and Baba zip up the jackets they borrowed from Catherine and Greg. It's about eight degrees Celsius.

'I thought you said this was the hot season in France?' Aama complains.

'Well, it's hotter now than in the cold season,' David laughs, and Aama scowls at him, tucking her chin into her oversized jacket.

'Why are we standing out here in the cold?' Aama asks, not for the first time.

'There's a party starting soon. In the sky. Over the ocean. With lights and fire.' I'm not trying to be cryptic, I just don't have the vocabulary to be more specific.

We stand on the beach in the dark for what feels like hours. Waiting. Waiting. More and more people gather around us, but still nothing happens. We shuffle and jump around, trying to keep warm, and Aama asks again why we're risking hypothermia on the beach at night when we can't even see the ocean anymore.

A murmur ripples through the crowd when the soft yellow glow of the village streetlights is extinguished. The beach is plunged into darkness and Aama and Baba turn around to see lights dimming and dying in the restaurants on the esplanade.

'What's happening?' Aama asks. 'You have load shedding here too?'

'No, you'll see soon. Look up.'

It's now so dark on the beach we can just make out the figures around us. There's an energy of expectation and the crowd falls silent.

The next noise we hear is a deep puff of air. It's followed by a whistling wail ascending into the sky ... then—

BOOM! B-B-B-BOOM! BOOM! BOOM-BOOM!

When the first fireworks explode into the night sky, Aama and Baba both scream and drop towards the ground.

40

Here are a few things I've just learnt the hard way:

1. Never surprise a seventy-eight-year-old man with anything that explodes.
2. Never surprise someone who used to be in the army with a noise that booms and whistles like an air strike.
3. Never surprise the citizens of a country recovering from a recent and bloody civil war with anything that might be mistaken for gunfire.

We thought they'd be all '*Chakai pariyo*, look at the pretty lights in the sky!' But we're lucky Aama and Baba didn't drop dead of heart failure right there on the beach.

When we first arrived in their village, the civil war in Nepal had ended only three years earlier. The armed conflict between the Nepali government and the Maoist communist party raged for ten years from 1996. During that time, 17,000 people were killed and hundreds of thousands of others were kidnapped, displaced and injured. Then in 2001, the country went into shock when nine members of the Nepali royal family were murdered—apparently by one of their own.

The official story is that a drunk and lovesick Crown Prince Dipendra gunned down his parents, reigning King Birendra and Queen Aishwarya, and most of their royal successors at a family dinner party. To put this into context, just imagine waking up to the news that a tragedy of this scale had happened within the British Royal family. It would be too horrifying, too *unthinkable* to be believed.

After the massacre, the prince is said to have shot himself in the head and fallen into a coma. He was proclaimed King of Nepal for three days, during which time the palace claimed an accidental discharge of an automatic weapon killed the other nine royals. A government enquiry later found that the prince, affectionately referred to as Dippy by the people of Nepal, was responsible for his family's deaths. Some say he did it because he was angry with his parents who wouldn't let him marry the woman he loved, while others claim it was because he was unhappy with changes his father had made to the monarchy's powers. All we know for sure is he died from his wounds, then his uncle, Gyanendra, became king.

While this is the version of events most widely accepted in the international community, many Nepali people I know have different beliefs around what happened that night. Some question whether the government investigation was thorough enough, or whether this story is a cover-up, but they've accepted the case is closed and we may never know the whole truth.

If you were alive in 1997 and remember the collective grief felt throughout the world when Princess Diana died, you may have some sense of how a nation might suffer when their royals are massacred in their own palace. The country went into a tailspin. After a long period of violence and protests, the Nepali government stripped the new king of all his ruling powers and the war ended with a peace agreement soon afterwards. The king was dethroned in 2008 and the country was declared a republic. The people in power have been playing musical chairs ever since.

When we arrived in Nepal, the conflict was officially over but the country was still in turmoil. The Maoists were staging violent protests and organising nationwide strikes to shut down and disrupt daily life. On random days, they forced all schools, businesses and roads to close and they set fire to the homes, buildings and cars of people who refused to comply. Once, during a three-day Maoist strike, we had a near miss with the rebels while eating at a friend's Tibetan momo restaurant in a back street of Pokhara. The Maoists were patrolling the streets in open Jeeps and trucks, checking to make sure no businesses were open or operating. The owner of the dumpling shop was alerted to their arrival by screams further down the street. She pulled the rusted roller door down just in time and yelled for all of us to take cover under the tables. We huddled on the floor, our arms over our heads, and could hear the Maoists tear down the street and set fire to a vehicle outside. When the streets were clear, we abandoned our momos, escaped out the back door through the kitchen and ran back to the safety of our guesthouse nearby.

That was just one benign example of the day-to-day violence Nepali people endured for over a decade. Why on earth would

I think surprising Aama and Baba with the sound of exploding machine-gun fire was a good idea?

'It's okay! You're safe!' I scream, trying to be heard over the fireworks exploding around us. But either Aama and Baba can't hear me, or they don't believe me. The only reason they're still on their feet is because Véronique and I caught them as their knees buckled, saving them both before they hit the sand. Their faces are now burrowed into their own armpits, their hands pressed against their ears.

'Please look up!' I plead.

'No, no, no, no,' Aama cries, her eyes scrunched shut.

'It's not scary, it's beautiful. I promise you're safe.'

Finally, Baba (whose deafness is an asset for once) lifts his head. All around him, pink, green and gold sparkly rain is falling from giant stars in the sky. He puts a trembling hand on Aama's back and gives her a little pat. She turns her head a little and un-scrunches one eye, her hands clamped against her ears, and looks up at the rainbow fire illuminating the night. Slowly, her face transforms from terror to confusion. Then wonder.

Every time the fireworks shoot from the ground, Aama's whole body jumps and she lets out a short, sharp 'Oooh!'. When the fireworks explode and shimmer back towards the sand, she coos 'Aaaaahh'. Unprompted and unconscious of the crowd around us, Aama is making the same 'oooh, aaah' noises everyone else is making, and at exactly the same time. It seems all humans—regardless of race, religion, dialect or age—all speak the same firework language.

That night I lie in bed, replaying the moment the first

fireworks exploded. I cringe at the memory of Aama and Baba cowering, terrified and trembling in our arms. Why didn't I think about how upsetting the noise of fireworks might be for them? How much do we even know about what Aama and Baba have been through in their lives? Are there other triggers we haven't thought about that might impact how they interpret what we show them here? Our Nepali is improving every day and we're together twenty-four-seven, so we've never been in a better position to learn as much as we can about our adopted Gurung parents. To do that, we need to find ways to start the conversations that are difficult to navigate in any language.

Starting with the war.

41

'Today, we're going visit some beaches and learn about the war in France,' I tell Aama and Baba at breakfast the next morning.

'World War Two,' Baba holds up two skinny fingers, his voice crackling to life at a record-breaking 8.13 am.

I raise my eyebrows, 'That's right, Baba! You know about the war here?' Baba nods. 'Well, today we'll take you to where some of the most important battles took place.'

'Good,' Baba says in English. He gives an emphatic nod, raises two thumbs and grins. This is the first indication that we're about to discover a whole new side to Baba today.

Véronique lives just east of the famous D-Day beaches, one of the most celebrated historical sites of World War II. On these beaches, the British military and their allies executed an insanely risky plan to reclaim France from German occupation. They sailed from the UK to Normandy, then drove 50,000 army vehicles over the water from their ships to the beach on floating pontoons. It was the largest seaborne invasion in history and played a key role in liberating France and bringing an end to the war.

'All of this was bombed and destroyed,' Véronique points to the buildings in the villages we drive through along the Normandy coastline.

'It looks fine to me,' Aama says, watching the rebuilt stone houses glide past the window.

'Before World War II, this part of Europe was quite poor,' I explain. 'They were still recovering from World War I, there wasn't enough work and many people couldn't feed their families. Then the Germans came and destroyed their villages, roads and homes. More than half a million people died just in France.'

Aama spins her head around in alarm. 'But we've let Germans stay in our house through the homestay. They seemed nice. They didn't destroy anything …'

'No, don't worry. Germans are lovely. A lot has changed since the war. France and Germany are friends now.' I cross my fingers to show how tight we are with our neighbours. 'There are no borders between our countries anymore. We can even work in Germany and they can work in France, without needing a visa. We live together peacefully.'

'They bombed your country and killed your people and now you let them live here? Like nothing happened?'

'That's right,' I say. 'We all just want peace.'

'This war must have ended a long time ago.'

'Seventy years,' I say.

'That's not long! Baba is older than that!' Aama turns back to look at the scenery whooshing past her window through the lens of this new perspective.

Within Baba's lifetime, France has been destroyed by war and recovered from poverty to befriend their enemies and become the thriving nation they see today. It's been less than a decade since their war ended, but what might be possible for Nepal and the Maoists sixty years from now?

For the rest of the day, we time travel back to 6 June 1944. We stand at the base of Pegasus Bridge where 181 paratroopers fell from the sky to kill the Germans guarding the canal. Aama and Baba are awestruck, watching the bridge creak and groan to life, lifting itself above the canal like an old man from an armchair so the boats can pass underneath. We move on to Arromanches-les-Bains where the allied forces landed and launched their attack, then we visit a 360-degree circular cinema where the story of World War II unfolds all around us in pictures. Aama and Baba are transplanted from the modern world to wartime France, from the trauma and violence of the battlefields to the eventual joy and triumph of a nation regaining its freedom. It's a sombre topic and I'm worried it might be triggering for them both, but Baba is switched on and engaged all day.

In fact, he's the most animated we've seen him since he left the plane.

42

That night, Aama has a crack at making *dahl baht* for the first time outside Nepal, swapping her lone kitchen fire for an electric four-burner stovetop. It takes her twenty-five minutes to cook a meal that takes two hours in the village and before we know it, we're all sitting around the table again with a glass of wine.

'*Santé!*' we sing to each other's health in unison, looking each other in the eye as we clink our wine glasses one by one, being sure to never cross arms, as is the custom in France.

When I say 'cheers' with Baba, I notice he has a sparkle in his eyes. A youthful glimmer on his otherwise weathered face. He takes a few sips of wine and starts mixing together the rice and lentils with his hand, free from the stress of cutlery. Lost in thought. Then he looks up at everyone around the table and clears his throat.

'I know everything,' Baba croaks.

Aama looks up from her plate and frowns at him. 'What are you rambling about?'

Baba looks at each of us one by one, his expression warm but serious.

'I don't speak much,' he enunciates carefully. 'No. I don't

speak much. I can't hear what's happening around me, so I stay quiet. But I know everything. I *see* everything.'

Goosebumps prickle my skin as Baba addresses the room, everyone stunned into silence. Hearing these words is like seeing him for the first time.

'Tell us everything, Baba,' I smile and lean towards him.

'Today, I knew everything. About the war,' Baba says in a slow, clear voice. 'I heard many stories when I was in the Indian army. We also carried the same bags we saw in the glass box in the museum today. I had the same mess-kit. Canteen. First aid. Shovel.'

He lists the inventory of his army bag in *English*, and our eyes grow wide. Baba chuckles, revelling in our surprise.

'You see? I know this because I had these items too. I know what they're called in English because I was in the army after the British withdrew from India in 1947. We used to carry the same things every day. In the army, it was my job to patrol the Burmese border. I was with other Nepali people walking up and down the border of India and Myanmar, protecting the Indian territory. I was never at war, not like in the movie we saw today, but sometimes it was dangerous. We lived in the jungle. Not in a city. There were no shops and nowhere to buy food. Life was hard. The military just took us out into the jungle and left us there. We were isolated from everything and everyone we knew. There was nothing to see in every direction but trees, trees and more trees.

'Sometimes the army flew planes overhead to deliver supplies. They dropped bags of food from the sky and we all had to run around and find them, then carry them back to camp.'

'Yes, I remember!' Aama's face lights up. She zooms her hand around like an aeroplane over her head and mimes the mad panic of people running in every direction, trying to locate these precious food packages. 'If we didn't find the food, we were left to go hungry.'

'You lived there too, Aama?'

Aama tilts her head, 'Just for two years.' This is the first we've heard of this.

'How long were you there, Baba?' David asks and Baba holds up his hands to count them out on sticky, rice-covered fingers.

'Twenty-seven years,' Baba says, raising his chin with pride.

'All those years in the jungle?' I ask and Baba nods. 'Did you come back to Nepal in that time, Baba?'

'Every two years,' he nods, flashing his wife a mischievous grin. *To make another baby.* Everyone laughs and Baba gives a satisfied nod. 'You see? I know everything. Even if I don't talk much.' Baba scoops a handful of rice into his mouth and finishes his dinner in silence.

There's no great, dramatic change in the days that follow. Baba still stays quiet most of the time, but something between us has shifted. When someone opens up and tells you their story, they're not just recalling events from their personal timeline. They're saying, 'I trust you to look at the crazy, messy, beautiful landscape of my life and accept me without judgement.' Children's television host, Mister Rogers, is quoted to have said, 'Frankly, there isn't anyone you couldn't learn to love once you've heard their story.' And it's true. This is the first time our relationship with Baba has delved below the surface of pleasantries. It's the first real, back-and-forth conversation we've ever shared, rather than exchanging smiles and a handful of words. Sometimes Baba remained silent for so long that—I'm ashamed to admit—I found myself addressing Aama and barely speaking to Baba at all. Now, after our journey into the war together, I feel closer to him. It's given me insight into the challenges he has overcome in his life; how being isolated in the jungle for so long might have impacted how he interacts with the world today. I now also understand his affinity for climbing trees and why he seems so at home up there in the branches. This new perspective changes the way I communicate with Baba and that probably drives him crazy. He's used to Aama answering for him, but now I won't let him off the hook. I'm bugging him all the time, trying to pull him into every conversation, to find out what he's thinking. Because now that we have a few extra pieces of Aama and Baba's puzzle, I'm determined to find out more.

43

Aama can't stop crying.

We've driven 120 kms south towards the centre of France and she's been sobbing the whole way.

It all started when we left Véronique in Normandy. We were getting in the car, preparing to head south to Beaujolais where Aama, Baba, David and I will attend my friend's wedding. Véronique is staying home during that time and will join us the following week.

When it came time to leave, Aama fell apart. She reached her hands to Véronique's face, then kissed both her cheeks and started to cry.

'It's okay, Aama, we'll all be back together again next week,' I said, trying to reassure her, but it only made things worse. Aama stroked Véronique's face, her whole body now heaving with heart-wrenching, uncontrollable sobs. I couldn't understand why she was so sad to leave Véronique for a week when she didn't get this upset about leaving her own family in the village for a month.

David pulled the car out of the driveway and Aama and Véronique exchanged a tearful wave before we rounded the corner and out of sight.

'Sh-sh-she,' Aama stammered, her words tripping on her sobs, 'She's all a-a-a-alone!' Then Aama started wailing, swiping at the tears tumbling down her swollen cheeks.

That was two hours ago and there's still nothing we can say or do to console her. We try talking through her feelings and we try leaving her alone to cry it out. We try singing happy music and cracking jokes. We try distracting her by pointing out all the fat cows and flat fields of corn, things that were *chakai pariyo* during her first week in France, yet still the tears fall.

We have no idea why she's crying but we do know that

when we travel—when we're disconnected from everyone and everything we've ever known—our emotions are much more intense. The low moments feel like we're falling into an endless black hole and the highs send us somersaulting through the stars. We can yo-yo between despair and elation just by hearing a few notes of music or catching the scent of a particular spice floating on the wind. This is all part of the adventure, so I tell myself not to worry. She'll bounce back soon.

When we hit the two-hour mark, Aama is still weeping gently in the back seat. She's mid-sob when something outside the car catches her eye.

'What's that, Laura Maya?' Aama breaks her silence, sniffling and hacking her emotion into the back of her throat and pointing to the sky.

I lean over to her side of the car to see the object of her interest and I grin.

'That's a balloon, Aama.'

'That's not a balloon,' Aama argues. 'I know balloons. I've seen them at parties in the city. You inflate them with your mouth. *That* thing is way too big to be a balloon.'

'It's called a hot air balloon and you're right. It's enormous,' I say. 'It's big and strong enough to fly with a basket full of people, like an aeroplane.'

Aama stares at me. 'You're joking.'

'No, I'm not.'

'You're saying there are *people* up there, flying in that balloon?'

'Technically, they're flying in a basket, but the basket is

attached to the balloon, yes.'

'And how do you fly a balloon? With a computer?'

'No, with a fire, actually.'

Aama blinks at me a few times.

'The fire is inside the balloon, above the basket. If you want the balloon to go up, you make the fire bigger. If you want to go down, you turn the fire off.'

'So, you're telling me there is a balloon flying through the air carrying people in a basket that they're driving with a fire, and somehow the whole thing doesn't explode and fall out of the sky?'

'Correct.'

The corners of Aama's mouth curl up ever so slightly. One stale tear rests on her cheek as she touches her forehead to the window and looks up at the *montgolfier*. Without saying a word, she watches it rise and fall, floating over the shadowed hills below. A slow smile spreads across her face and my whole body exhales with relief as I see her eyes are now twinkling not with tears, but delight.

That's the power of awe. Incredible healing can take place when we're overcome with wonder, when we're in the presence of something immense that transcends our understanding of the world. That's one of the reasons so many people jump on a plane to somewhere foreign or escape into nature when times get tough. It's not running away. It's running towards the feelings that remind us it's *wonder*ful to be alive.

44

By the time we pull into an Italian roadside diner to eat that night, Aama is back to her happy, laughing self. After we order our meals, I ask Aama to try to explain what she'd been feeling when we left Normandy.

'It's just that we've all been travelling together for nine days, but now four of us are going to your friend's wedding and Véronique is staying at her house. Alone.' Aama studies my face to make sure I've grasped the gravity of this situation. When it's clear I have not, she repeats herself. 'She's *alone.* In that house. David is here and Catherine is in Paris. There is no one with her. And her mother is in the hospital and, given her condition, probably won't come home for a long time.'

I bite down on the corner of my bottom lip. Véronique's mother, Marguerite, isn't in the hospital. There's just no translation for 'retirement home' in the dictionary of a language and culture that would never *dream* of putting their older family members in a care facility. It wasn't an easy decision for David's family either, but Marguerite needs round-the-clock care. When we brought Aama and Baba to visit Marguerite at the *maison de retraite* in Normandy—a region not exactly famous for its cultural diversity—the residents were a little shocked to see them. Aama and Baba were equally shocked, however, when they saw what terrible shape these elders were all in. Marguerite has two broken hips and a broken leg, on top of chronic respiratory disease and a heart condition. She's been bedridden for almost two years. Most Nepali people are unaccustomed to seeing their family members in such a fragile state because no one in her condition would survive long in Nepal. The average life expectancy is sixty-seven—only a few years older than Aama—so people die long before they become this ill. Yet, as we all stood together around Marguerite's bed, it dawned on me that she is only two years older than Baba, the tree-climbing globetrotter who travelled 10,000 kms to meet her.

Now I understand Aama doesn't realise Marguerite *lives* in that 'hospital'. A few days later we have a similar communication breakdown when we arrive at the gravestone where David's grandfather, René, is buried. When we get out of the car, Aama fixes her hair and straightens Baba's *topi* because they think we're going to meet David's grandfather who is homeless and sleeping on the streets. There's no word for cemetery in a country where people cremate and scatter their dead, and I don't quite encapsulate his current situation with the words 'last resting place' and 'outside in a big park'. Suffice to say they're shocked to discover homelessness is the least of René's problems.

'Aama, I know it's hard to imagine because you live with four generations of your family, but in our society, a lot of people live alone.'

'But aren't they lonely?' Aama's bracelets clatter as she reaches a hand across the table towards me.

'No, I don't think ...' I pull myself up mid-sentence and

take a moment to reflect on what she's asking.

I was single and alone for many years before I married David … and I was happy. I've always enjoyed my own company and need plenty of space away from people to feel balanced and sane. I guess I've never stopped to consider if my friends and family who live alone are also *lonely*, because it's not the same thing, is it? Véronique is one of the strongest and most independent women I know. She's got a thriving social life and I always got a sense that she *enjoys* living alone, but I realise now I've never asked her if that's true.

'Maybe,' I correct myself. 'But just because they live alone, it doesn't mean they have no one around them. Most people have friends, colleagues, family nearby …'

'But if you have family nearby, why do you all live separately? Life is expensive here, so it makes no sense that you all pay to live in different houses. If you live together, you can share your costs. That way you only need one house. One box to wash your clothes. One tiny car to cut your grass. One indoor waterfall. Why pay for two or three of everything when you can share one?'

'Sometimes we do that,' I say, thinking of all the times I've lived with flatmates. 'It's quite common that adults who are single and alone live together in a house with friends or even strangers to share their costs.'

'But why live with friends or strangers when you could live with your family?'

'Because if we all lived together in one house we would probably kill each other,' is what I want to say, but I don't.

I start tapping my thumb on the table, pondering Aama's questions so I can give her a better answer. I don't want to fob her off with 'that's just how it is'.

Why do young people choose to live with flatmates but not their own families?

Maybe because if we live with our parents, we have to live by their rules, so we feel like we're still kids, dependent on them to survive. We're taught from a young age we should strive to be independent. As soon as we're old enough, we're told to learn responsibility, get a job, pay our own way and take care of ourselves. I'd go so far as to say our success in life is measured by our ability to 'stand on our own two feet'. If we still live with our family, it looks and feels like we can't make it on our own, because we're not independent.

I flick open the dictionary and search for the word 'independent' and find the translation listed as *svatantra*. I purse my lips and stare at the word for a few moments. That's the same word we use in Nepali for 'free' or 'freedom', which isn't the same thing. But it's all I've got to work with so I give it a whirl.

'In our culture, people are taught that it is important to be *svatantra*. If I need someone else's help for my housing and food, then I am not *svatantra*. If I show that I can take care of myself on my own, however, I am considered successful.'

'That's impossible,' Aama argues. 'No one can completely take care of themselves alone. That's why we have family and live in a community, so we can all help each other.'

I don't disagree. I don't know much about evolution,

but surely humans wouldn't have survived for hundreds of thousands of years if our early ancestors had to singlehandedly take down every sabre-toothed tiger they came across. Our species has endured because we formed tribes to protect ourselves, because we pooled our knowledge, strengths and resources. For the tens of thousands of years until the Industrial Revolution in the 1800s, many Europeans still lived together as a family like they do in Nepal today. Then, about 200 years ago, people started moving away from their family homes, flocked to the cities for work and began establishing their own households—out of necessity at the time but now it's become by choice.

'How do you become *svatantra?* How do you afford it?' Aama asks.

'We get jobs. We earn money. We study to improve our work prospects. We make our own home and pay our own bills. In Australia, one of the first ways young people achieve *svatantra* is by getting their driver's licence and a car so they can drive themselves around.'

'How old are you when you do all of this?'

'I was fourteen when I got my first job. I got my driver's licence and left home to live with my friends at eighteen.'

'I was fifteen when I got my first job,' David adds, 'and left home at seventeen.'

'*Svatantra,*' Aama ponders the word. 'If I understand this correctly, your aim in life is to be *free* from your family. In Nepal, our family is our wealth. We all live together and when one of us grows stronger, we all grow stronger. But in your culture, if you live with your parents when you're an adult, this is considered a weakness. If you are not *free* from them, you are not successful, so you leave your family, you study, you work, you get a house and you earn your own money. You don't have to share it with them if you don't want to, and they don't have to share their house or money with you. You are all *free*.'

'Right,' I smile and the table falls silent.

Aama has nailed that summary but there's something about her little recap that doesn't sit well with me. Somehow, when the word 'independent' is substituted with 'free' it makes it all sound like a bad thing, as if we're only successful if we escape the shackles of our family prison. Whereas in Nepal, families aim to build on each other's strengths, in our culture it's every man or woman for themselves. Or as the French say, '*Chacun pour sa gueule*'. Every person for their own face.

I'm curious to know: at what point in the historical timeline did we start using our ability to survive without our loved ones as some kind of yardstick to measure our success? I'm not just talking about being 'free' from our families, but also independent from our contemporaries. Now no man should ever need a woman to cook for him, and no woman should need a man to change a light bulb. On the road to equality, with Destiny's Child as our backing group, we've had it drilled into us that we must be strong and independent, capable of taking care of ourselves in every way. A self-sustainable human island. Now when we find ourselves having to rely on someone else for help, it feels like a sign of weakness. We would rather run around trying to slay our sabre-toothed tigers alone, aiming to be everything to everyone else but also successful, happy, fully autonomous individuals ourselves. Maybe that's why the English expression 'burnout' is now in the French dictionary, and we've bred an entire generation of humans who have no idea how to ask for help.

Aama's eyes light up when her fries arrive and with a giggle she starts to devour her skinny, delicious potato things.

I'm happy to see she's feeling better.

Because now I'm feeling utterly depressed.

45

'You people are so lucky!' Aama says, watching the landscape change as it whizzes past her window.

Aama spends our car rides asking endless questions I can't answer about agriculture and crops—what's growing there? Who owns it? How is it harvested? Who eats it? Now, as we travel further south, the fields of corn she's seen around Paris and Normandy have been replaced by paddocks of sunflowers and grapes. Enormous tractors trundle up and down the fields that line the highway, and complex irrigation systems spray water over flawless rows of plants.

'Such healthy-looking crops!' Aama gushes. 'Lovely flat land, huge fields, lots of water. Big machines that work for you so you don't break your back. You don't have monkeys invading your land and stealing your produce and you have every vegetable in the world.'

'I don't think we have *every* vegetable in the world,' David argues from the driver's seat.

'Yes,' Aama gives a matter-of-fact nod. 'You have everything. If I had just one of these fields, I would be the richest person on our mountain.'

46

The sun is setting as we pull down a small country road and into the driveway of the Airbnb guesthouse that will be our home for the next three nights. When I get out of the car, I feel like I've stepped into a movie—a romantic comedy set in rolling vineyards where a staggeringly good-looking winemaker falls in love with a clueless American woman who's renovating an old chateau. Soft amber lights illuminate the ageing rough-hewn stone of the manor, which is wrapped in creeping ivy and surrounded by grapevines that tumble over lush green hills in every direction.

The owner, Charles, greets us at the door as if we were his oldest friends returning home from a long journey. With his warm teddy bear energy, he ushers us into his kitchen where he insists we join him for a meal he's prepared himself.

'I can't *believe* you've come all the way from the Nepali Himalayas and you're sitting here in my kitchen!' Charles grins and shakes his head as we take our seats around a small wooden dinner table covered with chequered cloth. He thumbs the cork on a bottle of red sparkling Beaujolais. When it pops, there's a chorus of approval from around the table.

'Tell me everything,' Charles bellows, leaning in towards Aama and Baba and fixing them with his creased, sparkling eyes. 'Tell me what you think of France and this strange world we live in?'

Charles' approach to communicating with Aama and Baba is so mind-blowingly simple and effective it should be rolled out as a global standard protocol for multilingual conversations. First, he turns his entire body towards them and asks them questions as if they speak fluent French. He pauses after every sentence so we can translate but he never takes his eyes off them. Then when Aama and Baba speak, he's fully engaged even though he can't understand a word they're saying. When we translate, he turns to us and listens before swivelling his rotund body back towards Aama and Baba to continue the conversation. This is cross-cultural dialogue mastery: a perfectly choreographed dance. It's the most fluid, easy conversation we've had on the trip so far, which is lucky, because what Charles has to say may be the most important thing they'll hear in their entire month travelling through Europe.

'Aama and Baba are subsistence farmers, so they're blown away by our huge, flat fields in France,' David translates for Charles. 'They say our farmers must be the richest people in the country. In Nepal, they have tiny fields on terraces in the mountain. They work hard for their own food and usually have enough to eat, but they don't produce enough to sell and support themselves. Financially, everyone's doing it tough. The trouble is we don't know anything about farming in France so we can't explain how things work here.'

Charles tuts and shakes his head then turns to Aama and Baba, his once jovial expression now serious.

'You listen to me,' he says, '*You* are probably in better financial shape than most of our farmers in France.'

'That's not possible,' Aama shakes her head. 'You come to our farms, you'll see we have nothing.'

'Just hear me out,' Charles raises his palms with a shrug. 'I think you would be surprised. A lot of French farmland is owned by foreign countries. America. China. And our local farmers are struggling. The only way to keep their farms running is to borrow money from the bank, but then they have so much debt they end up committing suicide because they can't meet their repayments. Trust me. Our farmers are not rich. Our *banks* are rich.'

'Really?' Aama and Baba lean towards him, resting their elbows on the dining table, 'French farmers don't own all this beautiful land?'

'Not many do, not anymore,' Charles speaks with passion. 'Not so long ago, if a farmer owned ten cows, he was rich! He worked his own land and sold his produce to the local people. He made good money and lived a good life. But then things changed. People stopped buying their food from local farmers and started shopping at the supermarket. It's just easier when they can buy their apples, meat, shampoo and a three-pack of underwear in the same place. Have you seen these monstrosities?'

Aama nods. 'Yes, the vegetables there are all huge and shiny, like they're plastic.'

'Exactly,' Charles bellows. 'And what kind of chemicals do you think they put on those vegetables for them to grow so big and look so perfect?'

'Can't the farmers just sell their produce to the supermarket?' Baba asks.

'It's not quite that simple,' Charles says. 'When local people stopped buying the farmers' produce, they *tried* to sell it to these big companies. But the supermarket chains want to buy in bulk. They don't want the hassle of sourcing their produce from ten small farmers. They want to buy all their produce from one big farmer who grows and sells ten times as much. Now everything has to be bigger, better, faster, stronger!'

Charles puffs up his chest and rises out of his chair, becoming bigger, better, faster and stronger himself as he presents his case.

'So what do the farmers do? They take loans from the bank so they can expand their farms. They buy more land. More cattle. More machines. More computers. More equipment. And do you know what else? More *problems*. Now they have two hundred cows, ten times as much land and a marketable product. But they're also up to their eyeballs in debt. While the people in their community duck down to the supermarket to conveniently pick up all their groceries in one place, the farmer next door can't even afford to put dinner on the table at night. They're stressed and tired and they can't afford to take time off to rest. Everything you see out there—all the land, all the cows, all the crops—the farmers don't own that. Not really. The bank owns everything. Including the farmer.'

'Ehhh,' Aama nods. 'Debt is a big problem in Nepal too, because people take out loans they can never pay back. At least we own our land.'

'Precisely. So, your way is much better.' Charles concludes, laying out his palms and sitting back with a smile.

But Aama isn't finished with him yet.

'Tell me about these machines,' she says. 'I understand people have debt, but their work is also much easier and faster than ours. We've seen machines for watering, harvesting and ploughing, which is all work we do by hand and it's *hard*. You can't tell me our way is better when everything here is so *easy*.'

I raise my eyebrows and grin at Charles, curious to see how he responds to this one. But he doesn't miss a beat.

'In France, a farmer's work is less labour-intensive, yes, but what if I told you these machines are making our lives harder?' Charles leans back in.

'I wouldn't believe you,' Aama laughs.

'Well, it's true!' Charles bellows. 'Before machines, we used horses to plough our fields. Let me tell you, those animals worked the soil so well with their hooves that our harvest got better and better every year. Now we do the same work with machines, but it destroys the earth. These tractors are too methodical and not thorough enough at preparing the soil, so we reap less and less every harvest. That means we need more pesticides and chemicals to preserve what we do grow. The quality of our produce is getting worse every year and our food is becoming more toxic.'

I can see Aama weighing this insight against the stories she's been telling herself since she first saw France's glorious, huge, flat fields of machine-harvested corn.

A few months earlier, I struggled myself to help Aama and Baba with their family corn harvest. Each day, Kashi and Rakesh spent long, gruelling hours in the fields, baking in the heat as they chopped down corn stems. Then they piled the corn into baskets and carried almost their own bodyweight up and down the mountain terraces back to the house. There, sweat dripping and covered in dirt, they overturned their baskets so the corn tumbled out onto a canvas tarp where I sat with David, Aama and a neighbour. Our job was to remove the hard, dried kernels from the cob with our bare hands. It was like forcing teeth from a skull with my thumbs and I only lasted an hour before my blistered hands bled so much I had to stop. It was hard to imagine all this manual labour was somehow better than sitting on a machine and pressing a button to achieve the same result.

'It's true, we use oxen to plough our fields and our harvests are good each year,' Aama concedes. 'We don't use any chemicals. But have you ever tried driving an ox back and forth through a field? We work our bodies until they feel like they're going to break.'

'But you are doing it for *you*,' Charles punches out each word. 'You own your land. You own your house. You know that every hour you work benefits you. It feeds *you*. You can look at how much food you have and know if it is enough to feed your family. A French farmer never knows how much his crops are worth because it's governed by how much someone else is prepared to pay for it on any given day. He has no control over how his crops are valued in a global marketplace. He looks at his harvest and has no idea if he can sell it for enough money to pay his debts and feed his family. Whereas a cauliflower will always be worth a cauliflower to you. You know where your food comes from and you know it's full of vitamins and minerals that keep you healthy. In France, there are not many vitamins left in our food and we are getting sick. And that is making our lives harder in other ways.'

'Yes!' Aama erupts 'That's right, people here are huge. And slow. They work their machines instead of their bodies and that makes them weak. Your old people are so sick they stay in hospitals. But my husband is the same age and he is out climbing trees every day!'

Charles jumps back in his chair in surprise, 'What trees does he climb? He can climb any tree he likes on my property if it makes him feel more at home. But I won't join him because, well'—he pats his ample belly—'I guess I own too many machines and eat too much food from the supermarket.'

He roars at his own joke and the rest of us join him. When it comes to self-deprecating jokes about bulging bellies, Aama and Baba don't need a translation.

Soon it's time to retire to bed, hearts warm with shared laughter and red bubbly wine. As we clear off the table and pack our dishes into the sink, Charles makes one last impassioned plea.

'You listen to me on this one,' he moves closer to his new Himalayan friends and raises a dramatic finger to the sky. 'You stay the way you are. Keep your fields small. Never take money from the bank. Bigger is not better. You're doing things right for you and your family. We, the French, are doing things wrong, and we will pay a high price for our laziness and apathy. Never forget that.'

47

'This looks like Nepal,' Aama exhales as if she's been holding her breath since we left Kathmandu.

After almost two weeks and hundreds of kilometres driving between flat fields of farmland, we round a corner and the landscape changes. Out of nowhere, mountains rise from the horizon, their peaks covered in a light dusting of summer snow. Instead of bank-owned corn and suicidal sunflowers, the roads are now lined with deep green forests of pine trees. We climb higher into the sky along the winding road, and Aama and Baba look down to the silver river flowing through the ravine below us.

'It's like we came around the bend and arrived in Sundara,' Baba utters his first words of the day with a big grin.

That is exactly why we're here. We have no plans for tonight and nowhere to sleep. All we know is we want to show Aama and Baba the French Alps, our mini version of their mighty

Himalayas.

So far, the car ride has been long and torturous for all of us. David was wrestling with a hangover, and I joined him around one o'clock after spending most of the morning still drunk. Aama and Baba seem tired and quiet, but I imagine they have a lot of new information to process after attending the wedding this weekend.

On Saturday, my lovable Irish friend Damian married his beautiful French bride, Lea, at a bona fide fifteenth century castle. The ceremony took place in a garden that looked plucked from the pages of *Alice in Wonderland*, full of the Queen of Hearts signature rose bushes and manicured hedges. Everything about the wedding was a surprise for Aama, like Lea's stunning gown, which was white, sparkling and figure-hugging, as opposed to the bright red and gold sari Nepali brides wear. Equally surprising was the giddy, googly-eyed giggles of a couple in love while exchanging their rings and vows, rather than two nervous strangers meeting for the first or second time on their wedding day, as is often the case in rural Nepal.

Damian and Lea were unfathomably generous to invite us all to their wedding, extending my 'Plus One' to a 'Plus Three' without ever having met Aama and Baba. After the ceremony we stood under an archway of vines and fairy lights, twinkling like a magical tunnel of fireflies, and sipped champagne with their family and friends. At one point, a crowd of inquisitive souls flocked around us, curious to learn more about these Himalayan wedding crashers.

'How did you two meet?' one of the wedding guests asked Aama and Baba.

Of course, I knew the answer but, as always, I translated the question for Aama so she could respond herself. Instead, she just stared at me, her mouth twitched into a half smile. There was a long confusing pause before I answered for her.

'Their marriage was arranged by their families.'

'Oh wow! That's amazing! So different,' the group responded, all moving in closer to hear their story.

'What was your wedding like?' asked one guest.

'How long have you been married?' asked another.

Aama started fidgeting as I translated their questions. She looked down at her feet and nudged a rock with her toes.

'I don't know how many years it's been,' Aama mumbled to her shoes. 'I was ... seventeen?' Aama looked up at me with a strange smile and I quickly ran the numbers in my head. I calculated she must have been pregnant with her second child when she was seventeen, if not already a mother of two.

'Really? I thought you were younger than that?' I'd clearly had too much champagne and I didn't pick up on her vibe *at all.*

'I know it's not good here, to be married so young,' Aama's voice was barely audible, but her eyes were pleading with me: *please don't tell them I got married when I was a child.* Yet still I pushed on.

'It's okay, Aama.' I placed a reassuring hand on her back. 'You don't need to tell them how old you were. Why don't you just tell them what your wedding ceremony was like?'

'My wedding was difficult,' Aama winced at the memory and shook her head. 'I didn't know Baba before we got married. Everyone was drunk and dancing and I sat in the middle of them all. People kept putting scarves around my neck and clumps of wet rice on my forehead. I was young. I was scared. I didn't know most of these people. I didn't understand what was happening to me. Or what was about to happen to me.'

A wave of shame washed over me. It was like the fireworks all over again except this time I was the big scary boom that triggered Aama's trauma. When I realised, I steered the conversation away from marriage and towards Aama and Baba's first trip to McDonalds, so we could explore less emotional topics—like lightning-fast food preparation and skinny, delicious potato things. From there, the night disappeared in a whirlwind of champagne, laughter and Baba learning all the moves to Gangnam Style. After watching her husband lasso the air and gallop around the dance floor surrounded by a crowd of cheering onlookers, Aama declared she could die now. She'd officially seen everything.

That one night spent dancing like an enthusiastic South Korean horse helped them work up quite a sweat, just enough to tip Aama and Baba over the edge of acceptable hygiene by French standards. The air conditioning in the car is broken and their weekly shower is still two days away. We've reminded them that 'Hot, indoor waterfalls are gifts from God, remember?', but they insist one should never be too greedy. So, I crack the windows and hang my seedy, sorry head out like a dehydrated dog, hoping the 130 kph winds will blow my hangover away.

48

I can't believe the good luck we're having. There's an outdoor festival in Chamonix this week and the place is heaving with tourists, but I manage to score the last two double rooms available in town—at a chalet on the outskirts of Chamonix. Relieved, I leave the tourism office and walk back towards the town centre to find my quirky international family. As I wander, I'm struck by the feeling that I've been here before. I know I haven't but there's just something that feels so ... familiar. Like home. I stop to look around for Baba's *topi* (which tends to stand out in a French crowd), when my eyes touch on a series of enormous black and white images. Each one depicts a snow-covered mountain and I recognise some of their shapes. Lhotse. Aama Dablam. Annapurna III. All mountains in the Himalayas. Above them, a flash of colour catches my eye. A string of Buddhist prayer flags, just like the ones hanging at Aama's house, runs from a pole to a nearby restaurant. A chalkboard out the front says, 'Try our Tibetan momos!'

Hang on, where am I again?

I find my family standing beneath a giant image of Mount Everest. Aama and Baba are staring up at the two-dimensional mountain in wonder.

'Why would they have photos of Nepal's mountains here in France?' Baba asks.

'People who come to this town must love mountains,' David

shrugs, 'and Nepal has the highest mountains in the world.'

'No, that's not possible.' Aama points to the real mountains towering behind us. 'These French mountains are much bigger.'

'That's because we're standing right next to them,' I gesture to Mont Blanc. 'This is the tallest mountain in Europe and it's about 5000 metres high, but one of the mountains we can see from your house in Nepal is Annapurna I. It's 8000 metres. One of the tallest in the world.'

Aama stares back up at the images and shakes her head. The mountains outside her home have been the backdrop to the biggest events of her life, but also every mundane moment in between. Aama's mountains are so ordinary they're invisible. I call it 'Paradise Blindness', when you've lived in a place of extreme natural beauty for so long you barely see it anymore. When a visitor witnesses the same landscape for the first time it blows them away, but a local rushes past it with their head full of tasks and worries, focused on an internal world that is forever changing. After sixty-three years living in a house overlooking the magical, mystical Himalayas, Aama's idea of paradise is the supermarket.

'Can't be,' Aama argues. 'Our mountains are tiny compared to this.'

'They're not!' I argue back. 'The mountains you see from your house are really far away, so they *look* smaller.' I turn around to look for David because I could use some help finding the right Nepali words to explain perspective and depth perception.

And that's the first time I notice it.

People are eyeballing us. We're used to the occasional sideways glance or double take we've encountered in the rest of France, but this is different. People passing by are grinding to a halt in front of us and *staring* at Aama and Baba. I know I'm tired today, so maybe I'm a little oversensitive and paranoid, but these people look shocked. Maybe even scared. One man almost gives himself whiplash snapping his head around to look at us. He's so stunned I almost feel like I should go over and check if he's okay.

'Wow, the people of Chamonix mustn't get out much,' I whisper to David. 'Are you seeing this?'

He nods, 'It's like they've never seen a foreigner before. It's a small town, I guess …'

'Let's get out of here,' I put a protective arm around Aama and guide her through the throngs of people. David sticks as close to Baba as he can without touching him, and we make our way out of town.

Our home for the night is a wooden chalet with handmade embroidered quilts and ornate French doors that lead to balconies with little hearts carved into the balustrades. There are uninterrupted vistas of the French Alps from every window, so while Aama, Baba and David all retire for a nap, I pull up a chair outside to enjoy the view. I watch the clouds creep towards the forest from the sky until a dense fog settles over the town and smothers the chalet. It feels like an ominous sign after what just happened in the town centre. In the looming shadow the air chills, so I pull my jacket around me and hug my knees to my chest. I flash back to six years earlier when we lived in the

Alps and I worked in the shop selling ski clothes. It was my first job in France and I couldn't speak much French. Occasionally my poor language skills upset the local customers who were disgusted to find an Australian woman 'stealing French jobs'. They waved their hands in my face and told me to go back to where I came from, that I wasn't welcome in France. Although there were only a small handful of these angry bigots among the thousands of wonderful French customers I served that winter, they are the ones I remember most. Now sitting here back in the Alps reflecting on what just happened with Aama and Baba in the town square, I wonder if coming here was a mistake.

49

That night, we take down an entire fondue restaurant just by opening the door. As soon as the patrons see Aama and Baba, they drop their tiny cheese pitchforks and stare at them, mouths agape. Part of me wants to turn right around and drive straight back to Paris where people don't look at our group like we're a herd of rabid unicorns. But we stay, and the following morning we buy tickets to ride the cable car up the mountain before making our way to Italy. To access the launch platform, we scan a barcode on our tickets and push our way through a three-pronged metal turnstile. David, Aama and I make it through to the other side without a problem, but Baba pulls the bar when he should push and when it doesn't move, he panics. In a flap, he tries to force his tiny body through the barrier but then finds himself trapped.

'Let me get that for you!' a chirpy voice sings out from a little booth. It belongs to the ticket attendant, a tall woman with a mop of strawberry-blonde curls who beams the biggest, brightest smile I've ever seen on a human in the morning. She flicks a button, tugs the barrier and beckons Baba forward to release him from his little three-pronged prison. When she sees the man she's rescued, she gasps.

For a moment she freezes as Baba shuffles past her, then she stands bolt upright and claps her hands together in front of her chest. '*Namaste!*' she shrieks, so loudly that even Baba hears her. He whips his head up to look at her in shock.

'*Namaste!*' he grins back at her, before turning to us with a puzzled look.

'This is just so amazing, I can't believe my eyes!' the woman squeals. 'Baptiste!'

She calls to another staff member in a nearby control booth and he pokes his head out. He looks uninterested for the split second before he catches sight of Baba's *topi,* then he leaps to his feet.

'Oh ho! *Namaste!*' Baptiste bellows, his smile as wide as the mountain behind him.

'I think,' Aama says, 'maybe these people have been to Nepal.'

'*Everybody* in Chamonix has been to Nepal,' the woman cries when we ask her. 'When all the skiing tourists take over

Chamonix in the winter, many of our local residents escape to *your* country.'

'Really?' David asks. 'Why Nepal?'

'Obviously we're mountain lovers,' she gestures to the walls of rock and snow around us, 'so trekking is a big reason. But we also have a lot of paragliders living here. So, when it gets too cold in the Alps, they go paragliding in Pokhara. Nepal is like a second home for many people from Chamonix. We even have a Nepali language school here!' The pitch of her voice mounts with her excitement until she's almost too shrill to be understood.

'But never, never, never in all my decades living in the Alps have I ever seen a Nepali person come here. For all I know, you may be the first people from your country to ride in this cable car. I just can't believe it!'

Now it all makes sense. The shock on everyone's faces, the prayer flags, the momos, the Himalayan photos. The speechless dropping of fondue forks. People aren't staring because Aama and Baba are foreign. They're staring because they're familiar. It's not racism. It's not 'Small Town Syndrome'. It's kind of like when you see someone you think you know in a crowd, but then you realise it's a celebrity and they don't know you. *That* is the complex range of emotions I've seen flutter across the face of every gawker in Chamonix. It's not hate or xenophobia at all. *Wow, why did I immediately leap to the worst conclusion?*

'You must be important people in Nepal to be the first from your country to come here,' Baptiste says. 'Are you royalty?'

'Royalty, huh,' Aama snorts. 'You come see our palace one

day, you'll see how royal we are.'

'You are always welcome in my country,' Baba's voice crackles and he dips his head into a bow.

'Well, we are honoured to meet you, your highnesses,' the woman says, returning Baba's bow.

From that moment on, Aama and Baba become known as the King and Queen of Nepal. It's a wildly inappropriate joke given the tragic nature of the royal family's demise, but one that makes Aama walk just a little bit taller.

50

When the cable car drops us 2000 metres up the mountain in Planpraz, Aama steps into her new role as Queen, proud to know she may be the first of her people to walk on this part of the earth. Now, whenever someone looks at us, Aama gives them a regal wave. At one point she almost causes an aviation incident, when a paraglider snaps his head around to look at them as his feet are running down a sloping cliff face towards the sky.

As we walk, Aama notices some thick steel columns erected in two lines up the mountain.

'What's this, Laura Maya?' Aama asks, pointing to the metal chairs suspended on cables between the poles. 'Is it for electricity?'

'It's a different kind of cable car, but with chairs.'

'Why isn't it moving?'

'Because it only operates in winter when there's lots of snow here.'

Aama looks back up at the chairs and studies them before turning back to me. 'But there's no protection. No roof. Just a chair. If it's this cold in summer, why would anyone use that in winter?'

'It's for skiing,' I say, thrusting my hips from left to right and making the swoosh-swoosh sound of snow being carved at high speed.

Aama stares at me. 'Is that another one of your wedding dances?'

'No,' I chortle. 'It's a snow sport. You put on lots of warm clothes, then you take two long, skinny pieces of wood and attach them to your feet. You hold a stick in each hand for balance, then you go wheeeeeeeee all the way from here to the bottom of the mountain.' I demonstrate the movement with two fingers running down my arm like a ski slope.

'When you get to the bottom, you sit on these chairs and they carry you back up the mountain.'

'Why?'

'So you can, um … do it again,' I shrug.

'Are you carrying anything down the mountain? Like rice or buffalo poo?'

'No.'

'Are you carrying anything *up* the mountain?'

'No.'

'So, you go all the way up just so you can go back down?'

'Yeah. That's right.'

'Why?'

'I guess, because it's fun. It's a sport.'

Aama holds my gaze for a few seconds, studying my face to decide if I'm telling the truth or not. I've never *not* told her the truth about anything, but I understand why we have to do this little dance.

When we returned to the village after our first long hiatus, Aama and Kashi told us stories about every volunteer who came after us—including a sporty Scottish lad named Murray.

'Every morning he would put on a pair of dirty shoes held together with rope and then ...' Aama clutched her stomach, already roaring with laughter before she got the words out. 'He just started RUNNING, all over the mountain, like he was being chased by a tiger!' Aama was laughing so hard she was gasping for air. 'But there was no tiger! He just ran up the hill, then he ran back down. For no reason. He wasn't going to see anyone. He wasn't transporting crops. Two months he was here, and I never understood what he was trying to do?'

The backbreaking work of a subsistence farmer is sport enough, so it's hard for Aama and Baba to identify any value in expending energy jogging or skiing if it reaps no practical reward. And without anything to compare it to, it's hard to explain to them the exhilarating adrenaline rush of throwing yourself down a steep snow-covered mountain in the middle of winter with two planks of wood tied to your feet.

We take the cable car back down to the town centre—Aama

waving at her subjects along the way—and we jump in the car for our next adventure.

To get to Italy from Chamonix we drive under the highest mountain in Europe which, for Aama and Baba, turns out to be quite a religious experience. Nepal is celebrated for its majestic mountains, but it is also prisoner to them. Countries that are landlocked and mountainous are at a distinct disadvantage when it comes to transport and trade, which is one of the reasons Nepal is consistently ranked as one of the thirty poorest nations in the world. Many villages in Nepal can still only be reached on foot, and there are no tunnels burrowed through mountains to assist with transport. On this day, the Nepali government doesn't even own the equipment necessary to dig a tunnel if it wanted to.

This is why no one in the car speaks as we make the twelve-kilometre drive from France to Italy through the Mont Blanc tunnel that was built fifty years ago. Aama chants her awe mantra '*Ah ma ma ma ma ma ma*', with every exhaled breath, but otherwise there is silence as we glide through the artificially illuminated darkness. We ponder the power of God and/or engineering (depending on who is doing the pondering), and how it's even possible that the mountain isn't collapsing on top of us right now. Then, just like that, the darkness squeezes us into the light and we pop out in Italy.

Then David swerves straight off the road.

PART 3

Italy & Switzerland

You have been assigned this mountain to show
others it can be moved.
—*Mel Robbins, The 5 Second Rule.*

51

When we come out of the Mont Blanc tunnel into an explosion of sunshine, the light hits David's eyes and incites a powerful sneeze that roars through the car. The vehicle swerves violently towards a concrete barrier and faced with impending death, we discover everyone screams in the same language; all of us hitting the same hysterical pitch for the split second it takes for David to correct the steering wheel and rejoin the road. This officially marks the end of our winning streak, last-minute hotel rooms and endless sunshine.

We are now halfway through our one-month journey, and everyone is tired. The summer days are long and jam-packed with activity, and we're spending a huge amount of time in the car. There's an emotional toll that comes with constantly changing environments and eating in restaurants, and it's compounded by a nagging guilt because we think it *should* always be fun and easy, but it's not. We'll look back on these days as awe-inspiring and life-altering, but in the moment, we're exhausted and daunted to think we still have the same amount of time left until we all go back to our usual lives. On top of it all, David is suffering from hay fever and looks like a bear who stuck his head in a beehive, and I'm raging with PMS. We know we're both tired and should be gentle on each other but instead we get into an argument at dinner over something ridiculous— how to order a pizza in Italian—and it spirals into all-out war. Back at our guesthouse we spend the night awake, hurling all our petty marriage grievances at each other in furious whispers, forced to express our anger in twisted facial expressions and flapping hand gestures while Aama and Baba sleep upstairs.

The following day, Italy responds by pissing all over us. It's the first rainy day we've had since arriving in Europe and the torrential downpours match our mood perfectly. Aama and Baba pretend they couldn't hear us ripping into each other all night, and we try to pretend we resolved our differences and got eight hours' sleep. It would be a great day to curl up on the couch in front of the telly, but we only have one day to explore Italy, so we suck it up, pull out the umbrellas and head into the ancient alpine city of Aosta, dragging our weary feet behind us.

To escape the rain, our first stop is a museum that offers a visual history of Aosta dating back several thousand years. There's one exhibition that captivates Aama: a life-sized model of what houses looked like in the Aosta Valley during the Stone Age.

'About 7000 years ago, this is what homes in this area looked like. When people were still hunting and gathering for their food,' I attempt to translate from the Italian information pack, even though I don't speak Italian. 'Back then, people used to cook over fires too, but they had to light them by hitting two rocks or rubbing two sticks together.'

Aama is entranced. She studies every corner of the house, her mouth curled into an amused smile.

'That looks like my house,' she says, her eyes never leaving the display.

I stop reading the description and look up at the replica

house. She's right. The thatched ceiling looks similar to her corrugated tin roof, and the terracotta mudbrick walls are identical. A ceramic pot like Aama's own water jug sits outside the front door on a straw mat woven by hand. It looks just like the one we sit on by the fire in her kitchen.

'We used to start our fires like that too,' Aama says to the house. 'Not that long ago, really. When our children were small.'

'Oh,' is my intellectual response. 'Right.'

'7000 years ago, eh?' Aama's smile is sad. Weary.

I puff out my cheeks and say nothing. We stand together looking at the house for what feels like hours.

When we head back out into the rain, I pray for another hot air balloon, a glimmer of awe to snap us all out of our funk. We get a brief chuckle out of Baba when David and I put our differences aside to re-enact a battle between a gladiator and a lion in the ruins of the Roman theatre. Next, David tries to help them reconnect with their spiritual side by lighting a candle in the Catholic Church, but I hide outside in the rain like a coward because I'm scared Aama will ask me more questions about the naked carpenter. Energy is at an all-time low, so we turn to carb-loading—eating giant bowls of pasta in a restaurant dungeon that's decorated with smoked pigs' bums. But all this eating, sleeping and looking at stuff is weighing on our Nepali parents. With no trees to climb, no farm to run and no feeling of purpose to strive towards each day, the sparkle in their eyes is starting to fade. We're walking out of the city when a huge clap of thunder rips through the sky and the heavens open like a monsoon. By the time we sprint screaming back to the car, we all look like we've been rescued from drowning in the ocean, gasping for air. On an ordinary day, I'm sure this comedy of errors would have made me laugh, but it seems we're too far gone. David pulls the car out onto the street and we're still in traffic on the outskirts of Aosta when Aama and Baba both start snoring. They sleep all the way to Switzerland.

52

When Aama wakes up, we're in another tunnel approaching the border. Her sleep is disturbed by the sound of me emptying the contents of my handbag onto the floor, searching for our passports in the dark.

'Why do we need our passports, Laura Maya?' Aama yawns.

'We're crossing into a new country,' I remind her.

'Switzerland?' Aama remembers, wriggling upright in her seat and craning her neck to see around the driver's seat. 'Are you serious, we're going to Switzerland?'

'Yeah, we'll be there in a few minutes,' I say. Aama grins and sits bolt upright. The frail, tired woman we left in Aosta forty-three minutes ago now looks alert, excited and ready to take on the world.

'How exciting!' Aama exclaims. 'Now we can find out what the tree people promised.'

The what?

Aama launches into an animated story, words tumbling from her mouth so fast I can't work out where one stops and the next one starts. I can tell by her facial expressions and enthusiastic hand gestures that this is an important story. A shocking story. Maybe even a funny story. But unfortunately, I can't understand any of it.

'Did you get that?' David raises his eyebrows at me in the rear-view mirror and I shake my head.

'I'm sorry Aama, I didn't understand,' I grimace and her shoulders drop. 'Maybe if you speak a little slower?'

Aama takes a long, deep breath and starts again from the beginning. She swallows her obvious frustration and pauses after every sentence, checking to make sure I understand before she keeps going.

'Last year, there was a big election in Nepal, remember? We had to vote for a new government. Before the election, many of the political parties came to our village to convince us we should vote for them, like the umbrella people, the fire people and the tree people.'

'Aah, the *tree* people,' I nod. Due to high illiteracy rates in Nepal, each political party is represented by a symbol. That way, people who can't read can recognise their party on the ballot form. Rather than trying to find the right name, they just tick the box next to the duck, the mango, the sewing machine or the glass of milk.

'The tree people came to Sundara and called all the villagers together,' Aama says. 'A man stood up and made a speech, saying "You should vote for us because if we win, we will transform your mountain into Switzerland." The problem was, no one in our village has ever been to Switzerland. Most of us had never even heard of it, so we didn't know if that was a good thing or a bad thing.'

'And did they win the election?' I ask.

'They did,' Aama is breathless with excitement, fidgeting in her seat. 'So now I will be the first person from my mountain to go to Switzerland and see what these politicians have promised us!'

'Oh, wow, that's great!' A nervous, strangled laugh escapes my throat.

I'm suddenly feeling uneasy because I've already been to both Sundara and Switzerland, so I know the tree people will never be able to keep that promise. Not in Aama's lifetime, at least, and she'll see that for herself in a minute. But we're already jammed inside a Swiss mountain right now and it's too late to turn back.

53

As soon as we pop out of the tunnel into Switzerland, Aama and Baba are *buzzing*. They're both glued to their windows watching the world whiz past them, firing questions at me about Swiss agriculture and industry. I mutter some vague answers about chocolate, watches, banks and pocket knives, because those are the Swissest things I can think of.

Aama is wide awake, gleefully shouting out the name of every crop she sees, but David looks like he's falling asleep at the wheel. I hiss at him to pull over before he kills us all and he snaps at me to just focus on finding us somewhere to sleep for the night. After a while, the car drifts to the right and, with a deafening crunch of splintered metal and glass, our driver's side mirror collides with the retaining wall at eighty kilometres per hour. That jolts David awake at least, but our nerves are frayed when we arrive in Lausanne with our mirror hanging by its wires, limp against the side of the car. The tourism office clerk tells us the city is hosting a trade fair and the cheapest price for two double rooms is 1000 euros per night. We thank her, take an accommodation brochure and start calling and visiting every hotel, hostel and guesthouse we can find. Each time David pulls up out the front of a hotel, I run through the deluge to the reception only to be told either there are no rooms left, or there is one available if I'm prepared to leave my kidney as a deposit. With few options left, we pull into a roadside campsite where I stand dumbfounded in the rain as the caretaker points to a grubby tent backing onto the motorway that we can rent for 240 euros per night. I am literally soaked through to my underwear at this point, but I still can't bring myself to say yes. Aama tells us she would prefer to sleep in the car.

There's just one last hotel in the brochure we haven't called yet, so David dials their number.

'I'd like to make a reservation for tonight for four people,' David says. After a few seconds of silence he pulls the phone away from his ear and looks at the screen.

'What happened?' I ask.

'He just said "No problem, I'll see you tonight", then he hung up on me.'

'Argh, you didn't ask how much?'

'What part of "he hung up on me" didn't you understand?'

Our personal war rages on for the half hour it takes us to drive the twenty soul-destroying kilometres back in the direction we just came, past the wall we hit and towards all the signs pointing back to Italy. Aama claims she has a headache and puts on my earmuffs to block out the sound of our hissing and bickering, while in the front passenger seat, Baba pretends to be asleep.

Everything is falling apart ...

When we reach the turn off for our hotel, we exit the highway and our car immediately begins to rattle. We've arrived on a cobblestone road in a medieval village nestled within a labyrinth of grapevines. The sandstone houses all have antique wooden shutters and terracotta roofs covered in creeping vines. The long, narrow village cascades down the hillside through manicured vineyards until it reaches a great silver lake so wild and immense it looks like an ocean.

'Oh wooaah,' we're all struck with hot-air-balloon wonder as we bumble down the hill through the fairytale landscape to the hotel on the water's edge. The sun even sparkles through the windows for the first time that day as David pulls the car to a relieved standstill.

My heart sinks again, however, when we approach the hotel

restaurant. The candlelit room is full of round tables cloaked in starched white linen. Each velvet chair has ten pieces of silverware and four crystal wine glasses laid out before it, and the cloth napkins are origami folded into elaborate swans. If tents on a motorway costs 240 euros, how many gold doubloons will this set us back?

54

The penguin-clad man who greets us at reception does not sound Swiss himself, but he does nothing to conceal his shock at the assorted collection of foreigners who have just walked through his door. He looks us up and down and side to side, but after what happened in Chamonix, I just smile. In fact, all I want to do is leap over the counter and hug him when he tells us that the rooms cost 238 euros per night—two whole euros less than camping in traffic.

David takes Aama and Baba upstairs with the luggage so they can change their wet clothes and get some rest while I stay with the hotel attendant to sort out payment. By now, I know his name is Miguel and he's Portuguese.

'What's the story with your little group?' Miguel asks with a shy smile. 'If you don't mind me asking.'

I tell him everything. How we had an existential crisis that led us to Nepal, and how we came to live with this Gurung family in their Himalayan village. I tell him about Anisha and the vulnerable girls who inspired us to start a non-profit organisation. Then I tell Miguel how we all came to be standing here today, wet and exhausted, dripping puddles all over the floor that he will need to mop up.

'You know, I always dreamed of doing something like that. Something bigger than this,' Miguel gestures to the restaurant next door, his eyes misting over. 'I was born and raised in a small village in Portugal. There weren't as many opportunities as there were people, but life was good and I never thought I was poor. I dreamed of travelling to Africa to help people who were not born into my privilege. I wanted to travel and connect with people and communities who lived differently to me, so I could explore new ways of seeing the world. Just like you. But to make that dream possible I first needed money, so I came to Switzerland and got a job. I just wanted to make enough money to help my parents and buy myself a house, then I would head to Africa. But once those Swiss francs started coming in, it was too hard to turn my back on it and follow my dream. This is one of the richest and most comfortable countries in the world and compared to the people here, *I am poor*. That does something to your brain, you know? It impacts how you feel about yourself. Everyone back home says I'd be insane to leave because there's still nothing in Portugal. They tell me I'm lucky to have a job and if I stay here now, I can return home one day and retire like a king. Now I've been here ten years, and my whole life has become about making and saving money instead of following my dream to pay forward the good fortune that has always followed me. Now you walk in here out of nowhere and you stand before me, and you're living my dream.'

Yeah, and I'm a grumpy ingrate who has been questioning all my life choices today …

'Do you know what that shows you?' I ask and Miguel shakes his head. 'Maybe it's achievable for you, too.'

Miguel takes a deep breath, 'But how? How do you leave behind all this comfort and security and go off to a foreign country with no idea what you're searching for, or what you'll find?'

'You already did it once,' I smile, 'when you left Portugal and came to Switzerland. And if it doesn't work out, you've got a cushion of money and ten years' work experience behind you now, so you'll never have to start from scratch again. Most of the time the anticipation of how difficult something might be is harder to deal with than the challenge itself.'

Miguel nods slowly. He doesn't take his eyes off me. 'But aren't you scared sometimes?'

'I'm scared *all* the time. About *everything*,' I laugh. It's my first real laugh of the day and it feels amazing. 'I'm scared of flying. And never seeing my family again. Today, after driving around for hours in the rain, I was scared we weren't going to find anywhere to sleep. I was scared we would have to keep driving to France and my husband would fall asleep at the wheel and we'd all be dead. There's always an element of fear. You just have to get to the point when the fear of *not* living your dreams is greater than the fear of the risks and sacrifices you'll need to make to achieve them.'

Miguel presses an emotional palm to his chest, his eyes

welling up. 'You know, maybe you had to spend hours searching for a hotel in the rain today because the universe was trying to lead you here, so you could find me and tell me that story. Because trust me, I needed to hear that today.'

The drama and frustration of the last two days flash through my mind like a movie montage. It felt like a run of bad luck at the time, but what if it was a perfectly scheduled sequence of events designed to deliver us here, to this hotel, in this village, in a fairytale region of Switzerland at precisely 4.57 pm when Miguel was rostered to work? All of that so I could tell him it's okay to live a life that other people don't understand. And so he could remind me that even on a difficult day, I'm still living someone else's dream.

With that thought in mind, I squelch up the stairs to our room to check on Aama and Baba and make things right with David.

55

After a much-needed nanna nap, we go for a pre-dinner wander on the lake.

'Look at the way the light is hitting the water,' Baba whispers. 'The boats seem so small and the waves are so big. It's like looking at the ocean, but then we can see land on each side, so we know it must be a lake. A grey lake, because it mirrors the sky. On a sunny day, it might be blue.'

He points to the landscape around him, but the most beautiful thing we can see is *him*. Baba. The poet who knows and sees everything.

We all stand on the pier for a long time without speaking, mesmerised by the orange and pink sunset dancing on the lake and the wild silver waves rolling towards the shore. David reaches his arms out to make the universal gesture for 'group hug', and I move in to join him. Aama and Baba shuffle warily towards us and when they get close enough, we pull them in for a bear hug, catching them off guard so they roar laughing as we turn them into a Gurung sandwich. Any tension left over from the day evaporates. Even Baba surrenders and leans in for the hug, rather than flinching away from our touch. He just loves to surprise us. Then, still laughing, we link arms and the four of us climb back up the road to the restaurant.

56

We're given a royal welcome when we step inside the five-star dining establishment attached to our hotel. Our new friend Miguel bows to the King and Queen of Nepal, then places a protective hand behind their backs as he ushers them through the restaurant and past the other patrons—most of whom are covered in bling and clearly don't believe it's rude to stare.

We're seated at the best table in the house and the Swiss elite watch with curiosity as Aama and Baba sit perched at the edge of their red velvet chairs, dressed in the same clothes they wear to harvest rice in their fields. They're both clutching their hands to their chest, terrified to touch the fragile crystal laid out before them.

'Two farmers from a remote village in the Himalayas dining in our restaurant,' exhales Miguel as he unfolds Aama's linen swan and places it gently in her lap. 'I'm honoured!' At the same time, Baba sees this and snatches the bird-shaped napkin off his plate, plonking it in his lap himself before Miguel can get near him.

Tonight, the royal court of Nepal are waited on by their doting subjects. When we order the house wine, they serve us from the top shelf at no extra cost. When it comes time for dessert, we order one portion of tiramisu to share between us but instead receive four huge, individual pieces on the house.

The restaurant is empty by the time we take our final bites of the delectable coffee chocolate mush, and the waiters are clearing off the tables around us.

'Thank you so much for your incredible service,' David shakes Miguel's hand. 'We will never forget the special attention you've given us tonight.'

'Well, we don't get many people in here with your adventurous spirit,' Miguel says with a wink.

'Yes, this restaurant tends to attract a lot of …' another waiter trails off, searching for the right words. 'Let's just say we don't see many people around here of different ethnicity.

People like us.'

There is not a single Swiss national working in this restaurant. Fourteen years earlier, one adventurous man from a small Portuguese village came to Switzerland in search of a better life. He found a job at this hotel restaurant and then, one by one, was joined by several other friends and family members. Now, like Miguel, they're all caught in this tug-of-war between the financial security of Switzerland and their longing to return home to their community and culture in Portugal.

When we explain this to Aama and Baba, they nod with compassion.

'I have one son working as an electrician in Dubai and one driving a taxi in Qatar,' Aama says to the Portuguese men and women now gathered around our table, all sipping coffees. 'I also have a son-in-law in the Indian army and another working in Saudi Arabia. Like you, our men all feel pressured to leave our country to find work, and now our women are going, too. It means we have a little bit more money in our pockets, but not much. Not enough to make up for our families being broken apart. Do you know what I would give to have all my children together in one room again, once in my lifetime?'

Our Portuguese friends nod passionately, and some press a soothing hand over their heart.

'I'm sure my mum must feel like that, too,' one of the waiters says and everyone falls silent.

'I've been in this country for ten years, yet I feel like I have more in common with you—two complete strangers I cannot even communicate with—than any Swiss person I've ever met,' says Miguel. 'Because most people from rich countries will never know the true pain of having to choose between giving their family money and giving them time. If you are born into a rich country, you're more likely to have the luxury of being able to do both.'

57

The following morning, we embark on a quest to explore mythical Switzerland and see what the people of Sundara were promised by their new government. To see the real difference, we start our search in the place that feels most familiar—in the fields of crops planted up and down the mountain. The neat rows of gnarled grapevines are the closest thing Aama and Baba have found in Europe to the terraced farmland that surrounds their Himalayan home.

'What is this?' Aama whispers when we turn a corner and she finds herself face-to-face with a tiny train. It looks like a bobsled mounted on a thin metal track, which stretches across the vines and winds up the mountain through the fields.

'It looks like a train for the vineyard workers, so they can move up and down the hill.' I examine the buggy and its different compartments. 'My guess is they put all their tools in the front section and ride up into the vines to work. When they harvest the grapes they could put the buckets on the back here to bring them down.'

I step back to let her get a closer look and see Aama's eyes are bulging. Her face is glowering. Her lips are pursed and I can see her pulse beating in her forehead. *That's new ...*

'Are you okay, Aama?' I ask.

'NO!' Aama bellows, and I take another step back. 'The Nepali government promised us they would transform our mountain into Switzerland, so *where is my train?*'

I've never seen Aama angry before. Not like this. I've seen her yell at Baba when he rambles after drinking too much *raksi*. I've seen her shout at Rakesh for ditching school. But this is an emotional rage.

'Where is the train to carry my tools up to the fields?' Aama cries, running her dry, cracked hands over the metal machine. 'And where is the train that carries my crops back down the mountain, so I don't have to bear their agonising weight on my broken back? What have these politicians done for us?'

Aama is yelling and laughing at the same time, overcome by the emotion and exhaustion of six decades of labouring in her fields with no respite. And no train.

'We need a photo of this,' Aama demands. It's the first photo she's asked for during the entire trip. 'So I can take it back to our politicians and ask them when they plan on installing my train in Sundara.'

Baba climbs up to sit in the seat of the train and Aama stands next to him, a stern and determined expression fixed on her face. We take about twenty photos from different angles, and Aama examines them to make sure they're good enough for a government shake down.

'You watch me!' Aama roars, holding a defiant finger in the air. 'I will go back to my village and show everyone these photos. Then, if after a while nothing changes, I will go to the government and confront these politicians. I'll say, "What have you people done for us? You talk about Switzerland, but do you even know Switzerland? DO YOU?"' Aama waves her menacing finger at an imaginary politician in front her. '"Well, I do", I'll tell them. I'll say, "I am Dar Kumari Gurung, and I have seen Switzerland with my own eyes, so I know that you have not honoured the promise you made to our community. *Now where is my train?*"'

58

'Who owns these ducks?' Aama asks, pointing her lips towards a dozen birds quacking at the edge of the lake.

'They don't belong to anyone,' I shrug as we stroll down a wooden jetty towards the water. 'They just live here on the lake.'

Aama's feet scuff to a stop and she places a firm hand on my elbow. 'Are you saying these ducks have no owner?'

'No, they don't. They're wild ducks.'

'Then let's take one home for dinner!' Aama's face lights up and she takes off like a roadrunner, sending the entire flock into a panic so they fly and waddle off in every direction.

'No, wait, Aama!' I shriek, breaking into a sprint, trying to catch her before she catches them. 'You can't do that!'

'Why not?' Aama stops and throws her hands up in the air. 'You said no one owns them.'

'Yes, but we're not allowed to take them. Or eat them. We have to leave them here on the lake.'

Aama turns and fixes me with her new trademark stare. It's an all-purpose expression of defiance and confusion I've become all too familiar with over the past three weeks.

'David had duck for dinner at the restaurant last night, yes?' Aama asks.

'Yes, he did.'

'So you *can* eat ducks in France.'

'Yes, just not *these* ducks.' I point at the naive flock of feathers now waddling back towards us.

'But these ducks don't belong to anyone.'

'No.'

'So who's going to stop me?'

'Well, no one. But you still can't do it. It's against the law.' I'm not entirely sure if that's true. 'These ducks belong to all the people who enjoy walking in this park.'

'And what do *they* do with these ducks?'

'Nothing,' I shrug. 'They just watch them. Sometimes kids come here and feed them.'

'It sounds like, in France, there are some ducks you feed, and there are other ducks that feed you. How do you know which ones are which?'

I puff out a huge sigh. Born into different circumstances,

Aama would have made an excellent lawyer.

The role animals play in our lives has been a hot topic since returning to France from Switzerland a few days ago. As farmers, Aama and Baba have a working relationship with animals. A mutual dependence. The animal relies on them to be fed and cared for, and they rely on the animal for milk, labour and some occasional meat. They keep an ox to plough the fields, a buffalo for milk, a dog to protect the house and a cat to catch the mice, and in exchange for their service Aama feeds them and gives them a warm place to sleep. It's a business transaction. Purely unsentimental. It's rare for them to even give their animals a name, which makes it much easier to eat them when they're slaughtered for a special occasion. The only other interaction they have with animals is as enemies, when they are forced to defend their crops and livestock against creatures in the wild.

In contrast, people in Western suburbia mostly consider animals as companions. For many Westerners a pet dog or cat is an important part of the family—a fur baby—and their needs and rights are considered in a similar way to a human's. This is also a mutual exchange, because we offer them our love and care in exchange for their love and affection.

However, the other major role animals play in many Western people's lives is that of food. Whereas Nepali farmers are mostly vegetarian, because of the cost and availability of meat rather than for religious or moral reasons, Western society has some of the highest meat consumption in the world. At the time of writing, a Nepali person eats approximately 20 kg of meat per year, whereas an average Australian consumes roughly 100 kg.

For the French, it's about 85 kg.

Aama is struggling to make sense of our hypocrisy because we have a deep emotional connection to some animals, who we'll play with and cuddle and even have sleep in our beds with us. Then, without a shred of remorse, we'll go into the kitchen to fry up other animals and drown them in sauce.

59

The confusion escalates when we take Aama and Baba to the zoo where they discover French people will also pay just to *look* at animals.

The Besançon zoo is built into a seventeenth-century citadel that overlooks the city. The animals live in enclosures within the fortress walls and inside what used to be the moat. We pay our entry fee and follow the path to the first animal display, but when we look inside Aama and Baba recoil in horror.

'How much money did you pay for us to come in here?' Aama demands, one hand resting on the stone wall of the Asian monkey enclosure.

'Ten euros each. About 1200 rupees,' David replies.

'But why?' Aama cries, slapping the air with an open palm in a way that suggests she wishes the air was a person. 'Why would you pay to see these filthy, disgusting monkeys? We should go get our money back!'

Personally, I love monkeys and so does David. One of the first conversations we ever had was about our shared love of primates after we both bought a piece of jewellery in Peru with a monkey carved into it. So, when we first arrived in Nepal we were excited to hear that monkeys sometimes pass through the village. I was much less excited, though, when I discovered the villagers greet the travelling monkeys by pegging rocks at their heads.

Whenever a pack of monkeys is spotted, someone stands up on a high wall and alerts the mountain with a long, wailing cry of '*Bandara aiyo!*'

The monkeys have arrived.

This sends villagers running from their homes into their fields, armed with big sticks, sling shots and even homemade shotguns. Furious, they collect every rock they pass as they storm towards their vegetable patches, preparing to fight a war. The first time we saw this happen, David and I sat in Aama and Baba's courtyard watching the chaos unfold around us in shock. We could hear people crying, '*Cha! Cha!*' as they hurled their weapons, then the rustle of leaves as a monkey scuttled away into the trees and out of the line of fire. They were stoning monkeys and I was horrified. Shouldn't we stop them? Surely there must be laws against animal cruelty in Nepal, right?

After a while I understood that these villagers are subsistence farmers and their fields are their bank accounts. They were responding to a monkey invasion in the same way I respond to my handbag being stolen. I know this for a fact because I've been mugged an above-average number of times during my travels. In my experience, when the assailant isn't armed, my natural instinct has been to fight back. The first time I was robbed, adrenaline surged through me and I held onto my bag with inhuman strength, screaming, swinging and kicking at the thief. I'd worked hard for the money in that bag and I needed it. Just like these farmers need the crops in their fields. Their food *is* their money, and if someone takes it away from them they can't go out and earn more tomorrow like I could. Crops need time to be planted, nurtured and harvested, so what would they do in the meantime? Starve?

Rationally, I understood this, but I still couldn't get on board. When the monkeys came to town, I skulked away to hide in my bedroom. Once, I saw a monkey swing right past me with a half-eaten potato in his hand, and I looked the other way and pretended I didn't see him—even though the potato patch he'd just raided was planted to sustain my Nepali family and me for several months. I no longer judged the villagers for their actions, but I didn't want to play any part in it.

Three years later, I was sitting on the steps of an abandoned house in the village. It was one of the only places on the mountain I could get internet reception, so I was sitting there alone, doing a university assignment on my laptop. Most of the villagers were gathered for a meeting at a house further up the hill and there was no one around, so, when a pack of monkeys bounded right in front of me on their way to our family's sugar cane plantation, I was the only one who saw them. Suddenly, I had a decision to make. Do I sit back and pretend it isn't happening like I've always done? Or do I race to protect the sugar cane because there's no one else around to do it? What's more important right now? My principles? Or my family's food supply?

Within seconds, I was gathering up the layers of my Nepali *lungi* and petticoat and sprinting after a pack of monkeys. As I ran, I bent down to collect any rocks I found along the way and when I caught up with the monkeys, I opened fire. It's important to note that I have never been much of a ball sports person, or an *any* sports person, actually. There was never any real danger of me actually *hitting* a monkey, which is why my rocks did nothing to slow them down. The monkeys snapped off several stems of sugar cane before turning to look at me with a mischievous grin. It felt like they were mocking me. Then they leapt into the potato patch and I was hit by an overwhelming wave of rage.

'*Bandara aiyooooo!*' I wailed into the air, calling for backup.

Then, lips pursed, I dropped to my knees and swept the dirt for bigger rocks. With a determined '*chha!*'—which I assume is some kind of magical monkey shoo mantra—I hurled rock after rock and, fuelled by fury and adrenaline, I started to get closer to hitting my mark.

If you had told me a few years earlier that I would one day be standing on farmland in the Himalayas throwing rocks at monkeys, I would have been deeply offended. I loved monkeys. I was a vegetarian. I could never have imagined a scenario when I would willingly try to hurt an animal, yet here I was, stoning monkeys, and it didn't even feel wrong.

Aama heard my screams as she arrived home and she

joined me in the trenches until we'd fought off the last monkey together. Back at the house, she poured cool water over the angry rash on my ankles from a stinging nettle bush I leapt through on my great monkey chase. Then, sitting cross-legged in the courtyard, Aama chopped up the half-chewed remnants of everything the monkeys had destroyed to use in tonight's dinner.

This was one of those sweet, psychedelic moments when— just for a split second—the barrier between our cultures fell away. I wasn't an observer, but a participant. My actions mirrored theirs unconsciously. We didn't need to explain ourselves to each other. Instead of two distinct cultures viewing each other from our own different worlds, we were standing next to each other side by side, looking out at the same world together.

By the time I was throwing rocks at monkeys, a lot of other world views had shifted for me. Squatting on a concrete floor in the dark and washing my hair with two buckets of glacier water honestly felt like a luxury; eating rice and lentils with my right hand felt more natural than with a spoon; and munching on the sugar cane recently liberated from the hands of a thieving monkey felt like a treat whereas, once upon a time, I would probably have considered that more of a health risk.

These brief, powerful moments are where transformations take place. When you live in a culture different to your own and you catch yourself unconsciously doing or thinking something that once felt awkward, abnormal or foreign, you build a bridge. It's a bridge that extends from the soul of your culture to the heart of someone else's. If we build enough of those little suckers, I swear, that's how we'll bring an end to intercultural conflict and achieve harmony and peace on Earth.

60

We didn't bring Aama and Baba to the Besançon zoo today to see the monkeys, but we do have a goal. There's a serious matter in the village that's been troubling me for a long time, and I'm hoping to find some answers here today.

Around the same time this monkey business happened, one of Aama's neighbours turned up at our house holding a freshly hacked buffalo leg. Buffaloes are usually butchered with great ceremony and shared among the village families every few months. However, on this occasion, the entire buffalo was missing except for one bloody shredded leg, which our neighbour waved at us as he approached with a nonchalant grin.

'Eaten by a tiger,' he nodded, tucking the hacked buffalo leg up into the awning of Aama's kitchen, as if it was the most obvious and natural thing in the world.

When we first lived in the village, no one ever mentioned anything about a tiger, or tigers, plural. But these days, they're blamed for all sorts of carnage, including the disappearance of our family's dog and the midnight slaughter of one of the teachers' goats.

Now the villagers insist it's not even safe to go to the

bathroom alone at night. 'You should always take David with you,' they warn me, wagging a stern finger in my face. What they think David might be able to do if we encounter a hungry tiger in the toilet in the middle of the night, I've never been quite sure.

No one in the village, or online, can tell me if we're talking about your classic Tigger-style orange-and-black-striped tigers, or just massive wildcats with bad tempers and big personalities. Our trip to the zoo today is an opportunity to set the record straight.

After wandering around the zoo for a couple of hours, we approach the tiger enclosure and Aama and Baba peer inside.

I wait for a response, but they don't say anything.

'This is a tiger,' I prompt.

They both nod in agreement. It is a tiger. Neither of them deny it.

'Is this the kind of tiger you have in the village?' I ask, screaming my question into Baba's good ear.

'Yes.' Baba confirms at the same time as Aama shakes her head.

'No,' Aama looks at Baba for a moment then gives him a playful backhand on the arm. 'No, it isn't!' she insists before turning back to us. 'That's a tiger, yes, but not the tiger we have in the village.'

'*Ho!*' Baba argues, 'these are the same tigers we have in our village! With the orange and black stripes.'

'No, they're not!'

'Yes, they are!'

They launch into an animated argument in Gurung, and we can no longer follow the conversation.

While they bicker loudly, a French family walking towards us gives us a wary look and takes a wide berth to avoid us. As they come past, one of their children—a boy who looks about four years old—looks up at Baba and points to the *topi* perched upright on his head.

'Look, Mummy!' he exclaims, excited. 'It's a Smurf!'

61

It's our last few days in France before we move on to a new country. Most of David's family are on holiday this week so we spend a lot of time together exploring the lighter side of French life. We visit a prehistoric theme park where we introduce Aama and Baba to the concept of dinosaurs, and they get their first taste of 3D cinema, swiping the air to block the asteroid headed straight for their heads before ripping their glasses off in a panic. We take them tenpin bowling so they can throw a giant ball of stone at a pyramid of little white bottles, all while this summer's hottest Ibiza dance tracks thump in time with the disco lights. It seems like a pointless activity, but Aama enjoys it because she's better at it than Baba, and Baba enjoys it because the bowling alley has beer. We visit a chocolate factory, go for walks in the park and dine in a Nepali restaurant one night.

Aama and Baba are stunned to discover French people part with their hard-earned money to eat a *dhal bhat* that's nowhere near as good as Aama's.

We spend an enormous amount of time together as a family unit this week—hanging out with David's immediate family but also his extended network of aunts, cousins, godparents and close friends. While we're sitting around Alain and Elena's garden dining table the day before we leave France, Aama reflects on all these different activities and the one thing they all have in common.

'In your culture your family comes together for no reason,' she says, gesturing to the group of people sitting around the table. In front of us are a dozen crystal wineglasses sparkling in the sunshine and three large wooden platters covered with prosciutto, duck pâté and apple-liqueur-infused Camembert. We're all just kicking back on a sunny Sunday afternoon, grazing ... chatting ... sipping bubbly Crémant.

'There's no festival today. No one is getting married. No one died. But still you all came together today for no reason. You talk, you laugh and you eat a lot.' Aama points her lips towards the half-eaten grazing platters on the table, her expression serious. 'You really eat a lot.

'It's hard for us to bring the whole family together because one person has to stay home to protect the house and make sure all our jobs are done, so someone always has to miss out. But not you! You can schedule your work so you all have a holiday at the same time, then you can lock your house as if it's no big deal and all go out together. When I go home I want to bring all my children together again, too. We'll never be able to take as many holidays as you, but maybe we can just come together and eat rice and laugh. For no reason.'

'We don't take *that* many holidays,' Alain chimes in. 'It's summer now so it looks like everyone is on holiday all the time, but we work hard most of the year. We only get five weeks off over the summer and Christmas time.'

'Yeah, so don't go back to Nepal telling everyone we're on holiday all the time!' a cousin laughs, and everyone joins in.

Aama nods enthusiastically as I translate, 'Yes, that's exactly what I'll tell everyone because that's what life is like here. You work a little, you take many holidays and you eat a lot.'

When we translate what Aama says, several of our friends and extended family members—who are meeting Aama and Baba for the first time today—sit forward in their chairs. What they've just heard is: 'You're a lazy bunch of gluttonous hedonists!' Which is, of course, the ultimate insult in Western society where many of us measure our worth by our productivity and wear our 'busyness' as a badge of honour.

'Hang on, hang on,' a friend leans forward, placing a firm hand on the table. 'We only get five weeks' holiday in the *entire year*. The rest of the time we're working very hard. Does she understand that?'

Aama nods, 'I do understand that you get five full weeks each year. Then, on top of that, you get two days' holiday *every single week*. When you live off the land like I do, there are no holidays. No days off. No weekends when you can lie in the sand or throw heavy balls at little bottles. The land never rests and neither do our animals, so we can't either. The crops always need to be tended. Firewood always needs to be chopped. We spend half our lives cutting grass for the buffalo just so we can have milk in our tea. We need that milk to keep our bodies strong because for us, getting food on our plates is more physically gruelling than getting in the car and going to the supermarket. Now I understand a holiday can be good for your health, but so is eating, and I cannot do both.'

When Aama speaks, she uses the English word 'holiday' which is also used in Nepal. This word dates back to the fourteenth century when a holiday—a holy day—was both a religious festival and a day of exemption from labour. In Nepal, when they use the English word for holiday, it still carries this double meaning.

In Australian English, however, 'holiday' has evolved to mean an extended period of leisure and recreation away from home, or a popular synonym for 'a week in Bali'. When we think of the word 'holiday', it conjures up images of palm trees and piña coladas at the swim-up bar of a beachside resort, whereas the word 'weekend' refers to the days at the beginning and end of every work week—the days we believe we're owed as a reward for our money-making efforts. We don't look at *all* our days off as holidays, but what would happen if we did?

'So, if you add up all your holidays every year, how many do you get?' Aama asks, raising her chin to the air.

'Most people on a standard work contract get two days off every week. So that's 104 a year,' says Alain.

'Plus the *jour fériés*,' Elena counts the public holidays. 'We have eleven I think.'

'And the five weeks annual leave, which is twenty-five weekdays,' adds Véronique.

David punches the numbers into his iPhone calculator then holds up the screen for everyone to see, 'so that's 140 days' holiday every year.'

'Which is what? Four and a half months?'

'Wow, that means we're on holiday for more than a *third* of the year,' says one of the cousins.

'It sounds like a lot when you look at it like that.'

The table falls silent.

Aama looks down at her hands and turns them over, then she holds them out for everyone to see. Her palms are like cracked desert earth. She has callouses so dry they've split into open wounds. It's now been weeks since she last picked up her tools and worked in the fields, yet still her hands haven't healed.

'These are the hands of a woman who is having her first holiday in sixty years. You should be happy you get two days' holiday every single week.'

62

To have survived fifty-one years farming a remote Himalayan village and twenty-seven years patrolling the Indian border in the jungle with a gun, it would have been tragic for Baba's life to be cut short by a ticket barrier in the Paris Metro. That's the unusual situation he finds himself in, however, when we decide to take public transport to catch our inter-country train to the Netherlands.

We want Aama and Baba to get a sense of what it's like to live and work in a big, busy, bustling European city, so they can see that our kind of work does come with some challenges they don't face in the Himalayas. We take the suburban train and the Paris Metro so they can experience being crammed inside an overheated carriage with hundreds of grumpy commuters wearing headphones, all pretending the others don't exist. It normally takes about an hour and a quarter to make the journey from Alain and Elena's house to Gare du Nord, but today we budget four hours so there's no chance we'll miss our connecting train. Aama and Baba are stunned and silent for most of the trip, their faces smooshed into the armpits of countless unsmiling strangers, adding to a kaleidoscope of human diversity they've never encountered in Sundara. We keep a strong grip on them, but still they stumble and fall while we surf the heaving Metro as it hurtles through the intestines of Paris. Despite their obvious advanced age, no one gives up their seat for them. Eventually, the sound of screaming, scraping metal gives way to a rush of air and the train spits us onto the platform. There we face one final obstacle.

The shiny new ticket barriers at Gare du Nord resemble a modern-day guillotine. There are two sheets of glass that slide open when you put your ticket in, then they slice shut after you walk through, threatening to chop you in half. How very French.

While Baba fumbles in his pockets looking for his ticket, Aama stands terrified in front of the barriers, holding a hand over her thumping heart. One by one, she watches people put their tickets in the slot then walk through the glass blades at just the right moment.

'*Ah-ma-ma-ma,* this is where I die,' Aama mutters.

'It's okay, Aama, it's safe,' I place a reassuring hand on her back. I mean, I *assume* there are motion sensors on these things to stop people from being cut in half if they don't walk through fast enough. 'Just do exactly as we say, okay? Watch first.'

I put the ticket in the hole and when the glass swooshes open, I step through to the other side. I spin around with a little 'Ta da!', but all I see is the back of Aama's head. She's turned around to help Baba find his ticket and missed my demonstration. Anxious, Aama is yelling at Baba in Gurung and he's turning his empty pockets inside out, getting flustered. Last time we tried to get through a ticket barrier, Baba found himself wedged between three metal turnstile prongs and had to be rescued. If that happens here, there may be no coming back.

'It's all okay,' David says in a calm, soothing voice. 'Baba, let's get Aama through first, then we'll find your ticket.' He positions Aama in front of the glass barrier and puts her ticket into the hole. 'Walk through now, Aama.'

Instead of walking through, Aama freezes. Her eyes dart from one glass panel to the other and she's anchored to the spot.

'Go, Aama!' David urges.

Aama doesn't move.

'GO, GO, GO!' David yells in Nepali to match the 'COME, COME, COME!' I'm screaming from the other side, beckoning her to join me. I don't want to reach through to grab her in case I trigger a sensor.

In that moment I float above my body. I can see David and me on either side of the ticket barrier both yelping at Aama, who stands like a statue between us. Our yelps become screams and, with a jolt, Aama wakes from her terrified stupor and shuffles, wide-eyed, through the barrier. As soon as she clears the glass, she stops. Then Baba sees an opportunity and rushes through behind her in a crazed flapping panic, without a ticket. He slams into her back with the full force of a rugby tackle and Aama stumbles forward. Behind them, the barrier slices closed with a rush of air, just scraping Baba's vest. The whooshing sound reignites their panic and they both scream and throw themselves forward. The next seconds pass in slow motion. A strangled gurgle escapes my throat as I lunge forward, my gangly arms outstretched, and catch them both mid-fall—just after their knees buckle but before their faces hit the concrete.

I heave them both back onto their feet as David bursts through the next barrier to help, then the four of us stand at the entrance to Gare du Nord, doubled over laughing.

'Are you hurt?' I ask them both, checking their palms and dusting off their knees for them.

'No, we're not hurt but we're making life so *difficult* for you!' Aama shakes her head with frustration and gives her *lungi* another pat down. 'We're like babies again. We don't know what we're doing and you have to teach us everything.' She loops her arm through mine and smiles up at me warmly as we walk towards our next train. 'You know, now I understand what it must feel like for you living in our village. When you first moved in with us, we couldn't understand why you didn't know how to do so many things we find easy. We thought it was strange that we had to teach you even the simplest tasks. But now, you have to teach *me* everything. Now I see we all achieve the same goal—we all eat and travel and wash and take care of our homes—but not in the same way. Like you said, there's not a right way or a wrong way, there are just different ways to do everything. You can't cook rice on a fire and I can't walk through a ticket barrier. I'll guess we'll just have to learn from each other.'

63

When we arrive on the platform, it seems remarkably empty for an inter-country train. I can't find a carriage number that corresponds with our tickets, so I flag down a conductor.

When he sees our tickets, his eyes bulge from his head.

'This is not your train! Your train is on this platform but it's much further down at the other end. It's far, madame. Oh, *mon dieu*, you're going to miss it. Go! Hurry!'

We've already established that I'm not a particularly sporty individual, but I take off down that platform like a cartoon cat with its bum on fire. I hit every conductor on the way down, shrieking 'Carriage 16?!', and each one waves me further down the track.

When a guard in the distance sees me coming, my crazy eyes bugging out of my tomato-red face, he spins towards the next train conductor at the end of the platform and raises a gloved hand for him to hold the train. This tiny win gives me the burst of energy I need to run harder and faster towards the first open door, my tiny red wheelie bag bouncing on the platform behind me.

'Please!' I gasp as soon as I'm within earshot of the conductor. 'Please, my parents are very old. They can't run!' I gesture behind me to Aama and Baba who are doing the best sprint of their lives up the platform with David.

The French guard furrows his brow and pokes his head past me to look at the elderly Himalayan couple running towards the train. 'They're your parents?'

I thrust my phone into his hand so he can scan our ticket barcodes, then I brush my sweaty hair out of my face.

'I'm adopted,' I exhale, dropping my hands to my knees to catch my breath. I've got no puff left in my lungs to give him a better explanation. The stunned guard gestures again for his colleagues to hold the train, and I'm hit by a tsunami of relief when Aama and Baba reach the door and we pull them up the steps into the carriage. Then I turn breathlessly back to the confused guard.

'Adopted, eh?'

'*Oui*,' I gulp. '*Merci*.' I place my palms together in the prayer position and bow my head in a decidedly un-French gesture of gratitude. It is the highest token of respect I can offer him right now but I'm sure he would happily trade it for an explanation. He's probably seen white parents with brown children on his train before, but a brown couple with a white daughter? It would be interesting to unpack why one of those scenarios seems plausible and the other is leaving this gentleman speechless with his mouth hanging open.

Huffing and puffing, we find our seats and collapse into them laughing, wheezing and clutching our chests. We've survived peak hour in Paris, a guillotine and an Olympic sprint, and now we're on our way to the Netherlands to visit Aama and Baba's 'daughter'—a Dutch woman who lived with them when she volunteered in the village library three years ago. Jennifer, who Aama calls Sonni because Jennifer is too complicated, stayed with the family for two months. Sonni, who I call Jen (so I'll stick with that from now on), is a primary school teacher in Utrecht. She's the most qualified person who has ever held the keys to the library and the children adore her. In her first week in the village the kids mucked up, taunted her and locked her in the library after hours. Once she escaped, she responded by introducing hard-line discipline with zero tolerance for disrespectful or distracting behaviour. It worked. The kids were shocked to find themselves removed from the library for even the smallest transgression and it wasn't long before they were whipped into shape. The students probably learnt more with Jen in her two months on the mountain than they did all year. I also believe she's the reason Anisha found her passion for learning and speaking English and, for that reason alone, I am forever in her debt.

Aama and Jen have a special connection. Aama took Jen under her wing and taught her everything she needed to know to become a good Nepali woman. Unlike me, Jen rose to the challenge. She learnt to cook *dhal bhat* and make the village yoghurt, *moi*. A concert violinist, she also learnt how to play the most popular Nepali folk song on a local string instrument called the *serengi*.

Taking Aama and Baba to visit Jen and her boyfriend Leon at their home in the Netherlands feels like a good thing to do, even though they're perfect strangers to us. Secretly, I'm excited that as soon as we arrive, we'll get to hand over all the responsibility for making plans and answering questions—not that the Netherlands is entirely foreign to me. I was raised with a sense of being Dutch. I had a close relationship with my Opa who came from Eindhoven, and I have a 'sister' living in Hilversum—a Dutch exchange student who lived with my family when we were teenagers. Although I can't speak the language, Dutch culture and traditions have always been a big part of my life. I visit the country every other year, but still, I'm delighted to sit back and let Jen take the lead this week. Hopefully she knows more about religion and farming than I do.

PART 4

The Netherlands & France

The opposite of belonging is fitting in. Because fitting in is assessing a group of people and changing who you are, and true belonging never asks us to change who we are.
It demands that we *be* who we are.
—*Brené Brown*

64

'You're putting me to shame!' I scold Jen playfully when we arrive at her apartment. She's serving Aama and Baba a vegetable curry with rice for their first night in her home, and they're excited to eat food that looks familiar. 'This crazy adventure started because Aama wanted to come to France to teach me how to cook rice, but I haven't set foot in the kitchen since we got here.'

We've only been at Jen's house for an hour but I notice there's something different about the way Aama is behaving here. For some reason, she seems more at ease in Jen's home than she was with David's family. Rather than sitting at the table as a guest, she's in the kitchen stirring Jen's curry and making comments about its consistency. She dabs at some wet plates with a hand towel and takes a quick snoop in the cupboards. We've offered Aama the chance to get involved with cooking and basic household tasks in France, just like we do at her home in the village, but apart from making *dahl bhat* twice she's always politely declined. But now in Jen's house she's getting into everything and making herself at home straight away.

Normally, when we sit at the dinner table, Aama and Baba wait to be served. We've told them countless times that in France we serve up our own plates from the food laid out on the table, but Aama prefers we dish up their first helping like she does for her guests. Then she takes care of seconds for her and Baba once she knows everyone else has had their fair share.

But tonight, when Jen places two large bowls of rice and curry on the table, Aama rises to her feet and reaches for the wooden spoon. Without hesitation, she dishes out the rice according to the traditional Nepali pecking order: Baba, David, Leon, Jen, me then herself. Then she surveys everyone's plates throughout the meal.

'Your husband is hungry,' Aama looks up at me and points to David's empty plate with her lips.

'Well, then my husband can serve himself some more food,' I laugh, but Aama gives me a strange smile. 'Remember, Aama? We all serve ourselves here.'

'Are you hungry, David?' Aama pulls rank on me. I raise my eyebrows at David and he looks from me to Aama, confused.

'No. Maybe. A little,' David searches for whatever answer will keep everyone happy.

With a satisfied smile, Aama heaps a small pile of rice on David's plate, covers it in sauce, then reaches for the bottle of wine. '*Raksi?*' She's never even touched a wine bottle before today but now she's pouring a large glass for Baba, David and Leon, then a smaller glass for Jen. When she turns back to me and tilts the bottle, four tiny drops of wine splash into my glass.

Jen springs from the table to grab another bottle but Aama waves her hand with great enthusiasm, her glass bangles jangling against each other as she says, 'We don't need another bottle of wine, Sonni. That's enough isn't it, Laura Maya?'

Aama looks back to me for confirmation and I bite down hard on my bottom lip. I do want more wine but I don't want to be disrespectful. So I shrug, Jen sits down and everyone carries on with their meal.

I'm not sure what's changed, but it seems Aama is suffering from 'revertigo'—when you revert to an old pattern of behaviour and it throws everything off balance. Is it because in Nepal the way a mother acts in the home of her son's family is somehow different from the way she would behave in the home of her daughter? Even though we are all foreign volunteers who came to the village as equals, could the family labels of 'son', 'daughter' and 'daughter-in-law' that we have been assigned really carry that much weight?

A familiar twinge of resentment tightens in my stomach, and I'm instantly transported back to the village: back to a place where women don't usually drink; where I feel torn between being myself and being a more conservative, compliant woman I think the villagers can accept and respect. But I'm not in the village. I'm 6900 km away in a place where women often enjoy a glass of red wine or two with their dinner without guilt or judgement. I do want Jen to open another bottle but I can't bring myself to speak up.

Cultural exchange can be a bit like playing a game of snakes and ladders. Since arriving in Europe, Aama and I have come such a long way towards understanding and accepting each other's differences, it's been like rolling endless sixes and climbing ladders up the board. Over the last few years and throughout this trip, our friendship has grown into the genuine love and affection of a mother and her daughter-in-law. I feel like I was almost at the end of the game, but tonight, I've landed on a giant snake that's sent me sliding back to square one.

With all the excitement, Aama and Baba hit a wall after dinner so we pull out the stack of bootleg Gurung-language movies we bought for them in Kathmandu. Jen sets up the laptop, I select a random DVD from the top of the pile and Aama and Baba are relieved to collapse onto the couch and escape into a film. It's the first time they've heard their native language spoken by someone other than themselves in almost a month. Once they're settled, we stay up chatting around the table and Jen opens a sneaky second bottle of wine. There's a lot of screaming and wailing coming from the Gurung movie playing on the computer, so it seems Aama is too captivated to notice.

65

The thin, huddled houses of Amsterdam stretch from a canal of glittering diamonds up to a flawless blue sky. Around them, the cobblestone streets are bustling with cyclists and tourists, meandering past shops selling giant wheels of cheese and bright-coloured flowers. Restaurant tables have burst their terrace containment lines and spilled out onto footpaths and bridges where people from around the world are sipping beer and laughing in the sunshine. Aama, Baba, David, Jen and I are among them, strolling through the streets, floating down the canals, soaking it all in. European summer doesn't get much better than this.

The only part of Amsterdam we avoid today on our great walking tour is the red-light district. While I'm all for broadening horizons and exploring the beauty in our differences, we agree to draw the line at the city's famous sex shops and brothels. There are just some conversations I'm not prepared to attempt when so much of our communication still happens in charades. So, we take the long way from Amsterdam Central Station to Dam Square via Anne Frank's House and arrive to find the Royal Palace heaving with people. There's a political demonstration in full swing with dozens of activists dressed in red, green and black. They're holding angry-looking Dutch placards and the only word I can make out is 'Gaza'. As a crowd gathers around the protesters, a ringleader screams something in Dutch then counts them in. On three, they all drop their placards and start singing, or rather screaming. *'Let me see your funky chicken, what do you say? I said, let me see your funky chicken!'*

Then the activists drop their placards and start acting like chickens, clucking their chins and flapping their elbows.

'What … is …' Aama trails off, her eyes following the human poultry.

'It's a protest,' I say.

'*This* is a protest?!' Aama and Baba snap their heads around to look at me before Baba adds, 'but there's nothing on fire.'

'What are they protesting against?' Aama raises a chin towards them. 'Chickens?'

'No, there's a war happening and they want it to stop. In Gaza. Palestine.'

'Ehh, that's where the naked man in your temples comes

from?' Aama's face lights up with recognition.

'Jesus, right! He was born in Palestine. Good memory, Aama.'

Aama smiles and gives a knowing nod as she turns her gaze back to the clucking protesters.

'Does this war have *anything* to do with chickens?' she asks.

'No, it doesn't.'

'But the protesters don't hurt people? They don't smash windows, set things on fire, block roads? Like the Maoists?'

'Nope,' I shake my head. 'They just sing and act like chickens as a way of getting people's attention so they hear their message.'

'Hmm. Well, it's probably just as effective so … I guess this is better.'

66

Our final destination is today's main event, a visit to Amsterdam's Openbare Biblioteek, the city library.

The only library Aama has ever seen is the tiny one we built in her village, with four cabinets of tattered books and one cupboard full of well-loved games and puzzles. Amsterdam's library, in contrast, is a glass skyscraper, and Aama is dumbstruck when she steps inside, spinning around on the ground floor, looking up at eight floors of books stacked above us.

'This whole building is just for books!?' Every level of the library is filled with bookshelves snaking in every direction. The total surface area is probably larger than the entire village of Sundara.

There are people everywhere of all ages, huddled against bookshelves, lying on couches and curled up in corners, each with their nose in a book. They're running their fingers along the colourful spines lining the shelves, or carrying stacks of books across the library floor, their footsteps echoing in the silence. No one speaks.

'What are all these people doing here?' Aama asks, bewildered.

'They've come here for the books,' I say, pointing at the shelves around us.

'The adults as well?'

'Yep, reading is for everyone,' I smile at Aama.

We stand on the ground level and look down to the children's area below where the bookshelves are laid out like a labyrinth. There's a mother and her son lying side by side on an electric blue sofa about the size of a double bed. They're both on their stomachs, propped up on their forearms, reading a giant picture book that has pink and purple monsters leaping from the page.

'What are they doing?' Aama motions to them with her lips, her tone lowered so they can't hear us. It's taken three weeks, but we've finally nailed whispering.

'Parents bring their children to the library to read books together.'

'But what's written in these books?'

'All different stories. It's kind of like the stories you see on TV—like the Gurung film you watched last night, except the story is explained in words on the pages and you imagine it like a movie in your head.'

'Ehh,' Aama looks up at me, 'do our books in the Sundara library have these stories inside them too?'

'Most of them, yeah.'

'So, books aren't just for education? Like teaching you maths and language and science. Some books are like movies on paper?'

'*Many* books are like movies on paper!' I smile.

'And normally, parents come to the library with their children? Together?'

'Yeah, when kids are young, it's good for parents to read stories with their children so they fall in love with books. A child who can read and who loves books can travel the whole world and learn anything they want from their bedroom,' I explain.

Suddenly, a lightbulb switches on for both of us. It's not one of those dull mood-lighting bedside table lamps, but a floodlight on a football field.

'Ahh, these books!' Aama grabs my arm as if we've just stepped onto an escalator. 'Are you saying they help you explore other places and learn about other people, like we're doing on this trip? So, these books aren't just for school. They're like a holiday.'

'Yes, exactly!'

Aama turns back to look at the hundreds of thousands of

holidays lining the shelves around her, and her eyes go wide with wonder. Now it all makes sense. Not just for Aama, but also for me.

It's been five years since we opened the library and, until half a minute ago, Aama still didn't understand the value of a book. She's always been Sundara library's biggest champion, offering to host us in her home while we built the resource centre all those years ago. Aama knew, somehow, those books would help the children in her village. But she never understood how or *why,* and we never explained it to her. We just assumed she knew. Why else would she fight so hard to make sure the library stayed open?

Jen offers to take Aama and Baba for a tour of the library and I take the opportunity to lower myself onto a bench and process what just happened. I place my elbows on my knees and massage my temples while the last five years flash through my head—every project we've worked on in the village, every meeting we've sat through, every night spent chatting with Aama around the fire about what was happening in the library. How is it possible we've come this far without explaining to the community that there is more to reading than textbooks, dictionaries and encyclopedias? After five years, many of the village children have fallen in love with reading, but now it's clearer why we've struggled so hard to get the parents and even the teachers on board. What if they don't know either that books can be holidays and movies on paper?

I'm still sitting on the bench feeling deflated when they return from the grand library tour via the bathroom.

'Sooo, did you actually show Aama how to use the toilet?' Jen asks with a playful smirk.

'Of course,' I shrug, insulted. 'We gave them a pants-up demonstration. Take pants down. Sit on the toilet like a chair. Pee. Or whatever. Tear off some toilet paper. Wipe. Pull pants up. We role-played the whole thing.'

'Well, she was taking so long in the bathroom, I got worried. I went back to look for her and she didn't lock the door, so I opened it and ...' Jen starts chuckling. 'She was sitting on the toilet like a horse.'

'What?' I gasp. We've been travelling in Europe for more than three weeks and I hadn't realised Aama was straddling the toilet and facing the cistern when she pees. In my head, I flashback to a motivational speaker at a seminar drilling the audience with the mantra: 'The quality of your result depends on the quality of your communication'.

'Oh my god, I suck at this,' I groan, burying my face back in my hands and shaking my head.

'Don't worry, it's funny,' Jen places a reassuring hand on my shoulder. 'It doesn't really matter, does it, if it gets the job done? So what if you didn't explain it right, or she just misunderstood. As long as you achieve the result you're looking for in the end, right?'

67

Dinner that night plays out much like the night before. Aama serves David a second portion of spaghetti when it becomes clear I will not, and I'm passed over for a second glass of wine when she does the last round with the bottle. Once again, although I wouldn't mind another glass of wine, I just accept it and say nothing.

'Can we watch that movie again tonight?' Aama asks when we stand up to clear the table.

'Sure, Aama, but there are five other movies here if you want to watch a different one?' David asks, fanning out the plastic packets of bootleg DVDs.

'No,' Aama's voice is stern, 'I want the same movie as last night, again.'

David puts on the DVD and the rest of us sit around the table chatting while the familiar weeping, wailing soundtrack plays in the background. I look over at Aama and notice she seems a bit on edge. She's sitting cross-legged on the couch, her hands clasped to her chest and her nose so close to the laptop I'm not even sure if Baba can see the screen. I can't understand what's happening in the movie but I can see a female character screaming and resisting as she's dragged by a group of men towards an aeroplane. Aama is hypnotised by the scene unfolding on the screen. Her expression is pained and she looks like she's trying not to cry.

68

The next morning Aama doesn't get out of bed at her usual dawn o'clock. When there's still no sign of life from their bedroom at eight o'clock, I start freaking out.

'Should I check on them?' I hover near their bedroom door. My brain has switched into full-blown catastrophe mode. I'm imagining them both dead in their beds, struck down by some previously undetected allergy to tomato basil pasta sauce. In my mind, I've already played out the scenario of having to notify the Nepali embassy and call their families to tell them we killed them with a spaghetti overdose.

'Leave them alone and come and have a coffee,' David scolds me. He's always Mr 'She'll be right, mate' and I'm Mrs 'These are the twenty-eight different ways this situation could go horribly wrong'. 'They're tired. They're finally relaxing into their holiday. Just let them sleep.'

But when Aama emerges from her room around half past eight, it's clear she hasn't slept at all. Dishevelled and exhausted, the lines on her face have become deep crevices.

'Are you alright, Aama?' I place a gentle hand on her shoulder and guide her to the breakfast table next to Baba.

Aama shakes her head slightly and I immediately start to panic again. In the five years I've known Aama, she's *always* been alright, even when she's clearly not. I've seen her stung by bees on her eyes and ears so her face was swollen shut, but still she insisted she was fine.

'Are you feeling sick?'

'No,' Aama forces a weak laugh. 'I've been on an aeroplane.'

Oh God, is she having a stroke?

'I know, Aama. You mean the planes from Kathmandu to Paris?'

'No,' Aama shakes her head and looks up at me with tired eyes. 'The plane they forced me to take when I married Baba. Just like the girl in the movie last night.'

'It's okay.' *Could my voice get any more high-pitched?* 'You're okay. Did you remember something last night?'

Aama gives a meek nod and David places a steaming mug of tea in front of her. He's getting on board my worry train now as Aama blinks and stares into the cup. She watches the water darken for a few moments, then she gives the teabag a half-hearted dunk.

'Just take your time,' I say. 'Then tell us what happened, when you're ready.'

'I was so tired I went straight to sleep last night. I kept having these terrible dreams, that I was being forced into an aeroplane and I was screaming and crying like the woman in the movie. Then I woke up and remembered something. Actually, I remembered everything. I was the one screaming and crying. But it wasn't a dream or a movie. It was a memory of what happened to me.'

'All of this happened when you got married?'

Aama nods, looking over at Baba. He looks back at her, his eyes a mix of emotions I can't decipher. He doesn't move or speak, and he seems worried. He doesn't take his eyes off his wife.

'Start from the beginning, Aama.'

69

'I got married,' Aama begins in a small but determined voice. She turns to Baba, her glass bracelets clinking together as she places a hand on the table in front of him. 'How old was I when we got married?'

'How old were you?' Baba clears his throat.

'Was I fourteen or fifteen?'

'Fifteen, I think.' Baba's voice rattles.

'When I was about fifteen and Baba was around thirty years old, our families arranged our marriage. That's when I was brought to Sundara from my village on a different mountain. As you know, the wedding was very difficult for me. I didn't know these people, and I didn't know what was going on. Baba was in the army in India and after the wedding, I said I didn't want to go live with him there, but his family told me I had no choice. Baba was married before, you see, but his first wife couldn't produce any children. They were together for more than ten years and she didn't fall pregnant once. They were allowed to divorce, which is unusual in Nepal, so he could be married to someone younger who could have children. They chose me. His parents wanted grandchildren, so they told me I had to go with Baba to India. I told them again I wanted to stay in Nepal and there was a big fight.

'They took me to the city and they forced me into this thing like a bus. I didn't know what it was, but I was screaming and crying and fighting them off because I knew it would take me away from Nepal. They locked me inside and I cried and cried until we reached India. I felt like I couldn't breathe. When I watched the movie last night and the night before, it felt so familiar. Like I'd heard this story before. Then I realised it might not have been a bus that took me to India almost fifty years ago. I think it was a plane.

'I went to live in the jungle at Baba's army base for two years. There was nothing there except trees. No cities, no villages, just jungle all around us. Like we told you, there was nothing to eat. No shops. Just these food bundles the army would drop around the camps from the plane. Baba was out patrolling the India–Burma border and I stayed back at the camp with the other Nepali families. They were good people and we became friends. Baba came and went from the camp and eventually I fell pregnant.

'I gave birth to Chija in India, but she wasn't a healthy baby. She was sick a lot. Then one day she got so sick she couldn't breathe. She turned blue and I was terrified she was going to die. The army arranged to have me removed from India and brought back to Nepal for her medical treatment. I think they sent me on another plane, but I didn't remember that time either. I just remember crying the whole way, scared Chija would die before we made it back to Nepal. She wasn't getting enough air and I was distraught, just trying to keep her alive.

'The doctors in Nepal told me Chija had asthma and gave her some medication. She seemed to get better and everyone in Baba's family told me I had to take her back to India. But by then I was pregnant with my second child, and I decided I wasn't going anywhere. I put my foot down and refused to leave Nepal. Baba's family weren't happy about it but they agreed to let me stay in the village. They had one grandchild now, and one on the way.

'I was maybe seventeen by then and I had to work hard to be accepted by the family. I knew if I didn't want to be sent back to India, I had to show them that I could be the perfect woman and the perfect wife, so I cooked the best *dhal* and I cleaned my house the best. I worked hard in the fields. There was a huge expectation on me to produce a lot of children, otherwise I would bring great shame on the family. But Baba came back from the army every two years to visit, and I produced seven children in total. Four boys and three girls. His ex-wife also remarried and had five children herself! Can you believe it? I worked hard and I made sure I did everything right so I could earn my place in their lives.

'In the end, I didn't just earn my place in the family. I earned my place in the village. People started coming to me for advice, for support with different issues. Slowly, they realised my ideas were good, my thoughts were good, and they started to value my opinion. I never learnt to read or write, but soon I was on all the committees—the mothers committee, the school committee, the village development committee. I wanted to learn to read. I took an adult class at the school for a while, but in the end it didn't matter. I could stand up in front of a group of people and say things that made sense, things that made people listen. So more and more I felt confident to speak up and to do things to help our community.'

'She made a name for herself!' Baba comes to life, his eyes glimmering with pride. 'My wife became the most powerful woman in the village. She's number one. The chief!'

He beams at Aama and she grins up at him, their eyes locked in an affectionate gaze. In this moment, they're so obviously in love. Even if that love was born from a trauma, locked away in the dungeon of Aama's memory for half a century. Until today.

Telling her story seems to lift a burden Aama may not have even known she was carrying. She turns her attention to the fried eggs Jen and Leon have prepared for her breakfast and asks, 'Did these come from the protesters in the city yesterday?' Then she cracks up at her own joke and we all join in.

Sitting before us at the breakfast table is not just a village chief, but a child who was forced to marry a man twice her age and transform her suffering into a triumph. Aama had to fight to keep her own children alive when she was only a child herself. Not only did she have to conform to her in-laws' expectations of her, she had to exceed them to be accepted on the mountain she now calls home. I've only ever known Aama as a total powerhouse, so I'd never even considered there was a time when she was meek, vulnerable, scared and submissive, that she'd struggled to belong in the community she now leads.

Maybe that's why Aama was always baffled by my resistance to being a good, traditional woman. Maybe that's why she's been so invested in helping me conform to their ways. Those markers of womanhood were the rungs on the ladder she had to climb to be accepted and respected in her village. These were the tests she had to pass in order to feel like she belonged in Sundara—a community that could either adopt her or reject her because she was an outsider. Like me. Maybe that's why she wants me to be the best Nepali woman I can be. Not because she wants me to change who I am, but so I'll be accepted in Sundara, too.

70

If books are movies on paper, then this is the part where we skip to a 1980s movie montage, like in *The Karate Kid.*

Imagine a fun, uplifting song playing in the background as you watch Baba entranced by a train station vending machine, jumping back in shocked delight every time he puts a coin into one slot and a bag of chips leaps off the shelf into another.

Next, you see Aama and Baba trudging through steaming cow paddies on a dairy farm, exploring a factory where they watch ten holy cows get milked by machines in the same time it would take them to milk one buffalo. They're crouched on the factory floor at udder level, watching the sacred animals move through the production line, trying to work out if this is genius or blasphemy.

Then, you follow us to a bee farm where we learn about commercial honey harvesting—everyone decked out in homemade beekeeper outfits which I almost refuse to wear because they look a bit too much like the hoods worn by the Ku Klux Klan.

The music kicks up a notch as David and I abandon Aama and Baba for the first time, overnight. With six people and only five seats in Jen's car, we leave them for twenty-four hours so they can travel to the UNESCO World Heritage site of Kinderdijk. We're standing in a car park about to go our separate ways, and David and I are *freaking out* like parents leaving their newborn with a babysitter. As our bus arrives and we run to catch it, we're still yelling frantic instructions over our shoulders, while Jen waves us off and tells us she's got it all under control. Then we rumble away on the bus in silence, wracked with guilt, feeling like we've had a limb chopped off.

The movie montage crosses to Aama and Baba the next day, sitting in the back seat of the car, marvelling at the traditional windmills that line the waterways in the countryside.

Next, you flash to a scene of David and me—alone for the first time in over a month—wearing white fluffy bathrobes and resting our exhausted brains on a mountain of pillows in a Dutch hotel. We're watching *The Smurfs*, giggling, covered in the orange dust of ten empty cheese ball packets.

The montage music continues as we cross to a primary school classroom where thirty wide-eyed and curious eight year olds are staring at Aama and Baba's funny clothes. Aama and Baba are staring back, equally fascinated by the rows of quiet children pointing at the roof whenever they wish to speak. When Jen shows Aama the 'conflict resolution' room, where children come together to work out their disagreements peacefully, Aama suggests it might just be easier to put a giant stone in each of their mouths and make them stand on one leg with their arms stretched out to the side. Same result, Aama suggests, without all the blah blah.

Finally, we follow the music to a modern home in Hilversum where David, Aama, Baba and I are having dinner with my lovable Dutch 'sister', Eefke, and her warm, softly spoken Spanish partner, Felipe. Eefke and I are dancing around the kitchen wearing polka dot aprons and wielding knives and wooden spoons, co-cooking my first meal for Aama and Baba since arriving in Europe. As the music starts to fade, I pull a pasta bake from the oven and glide out of the kitchen, gripping it between two oven mitts. A cheer goes up from everyone around the table and, as we all sit down to eat, the eighties movie montage ends.

Wax on, wax off …

71

'Hmm,' Aama murmurs, mashing the rich tomato pasta and melted cheese in her mouth, 'Laura Maya's first cooking is delicious!'

I shoot a grateful look at Eefke. We both know I only chopped a few onions and tomatoes but she's happy to let me steal the glory.

As everyone finishes their meal, Aama raises a chin in my direction and points at Felipe and David's empty plates with her lips. After a quick translation, Eefke leans in to reassure Aama.

'Don't worry, Aama. In our country, the women do not wait on the men. They can take care of themselves,' she laughs.

'I think that's good!' Aama says, holding up her thumbs and punching out the word 'good' in English.

I raise my eyebrows as Aama gives a passionate endorsement for the exact same practice she's been actively defying all week.

'In Nepal, I cook, but I don't eat until everyone else is satisfied. Sometimes, there's not enough so I have to make myself a plate of slop.' As I translate, I explain 'slop' is a mix of grain and cold water that creates a pile of stodgy, tasteless gloop often given to dogs. Eefke and Felipe's eyes widen.

'Every day I cook a meal in the morning while I'm running around, working in the house and garden at the same time. Everyone is working out in the fields and often they take a long time to come back, but I won't eat until everyone else has eaten. By the time they arrive, wash their hands and feet and finish their food, I'm so hungry! But still I wait. My family is big and sometimes, if the crops don't grow well, there's not enough food to go around. So, as their mother, I want to make sure everyone else is taken care of first. If they finish their plates and need more, then there might not be anything left for me when they're done.' Aama scrunches up her face and grips her stomach in a gesture that needs no translation. Then she laughs and shrugs her shoulders, '*Ke garne?* One of my favourite things about Europe is you all eat together. You share your food at the same time so everyone gets a fair portion, and if you're still hungry you share what's left. I'll miss that when I go home.'

Aama picks up the bottle of wine we brought and pours a second glass for Baba, Felipe and David. Then when she tilts the bottle over my glass, just the last little trickle comes out. I drop my chin into my chest and let out a whimper disguised as a laugh. We're stuck on a loop.

Like Jen, Eefke leaps up to get another bottle of wine and Aama waves her hand, her bangles jangling in the air like a warning siren.

'It's okay, we don't need any more wine.' Aama looks over at me for confirmation, 'Do we, Laura Maya?'

Eefke, who is five months pregnant and not drinking at all, holds up a new bottle of wine, 'Laura?'

It's remarkable how many thoughts can tumble through one mind in a fraction of a second. It strikes me how bizarre it is for me, an Australian, to be sitting in the Netherlands with a Dutch woman I love like a sister, even though we're not related at all. While at the same time, I'm adapting my behaviour to conform to the expectations of a Nepali woman who I love and respect as a mother figure, but I'm not related to her, either.

It might seem like I'm trying to fill some kind of gap or replace my own family through these relationships, but it's *because* I'm so close to my own family in Australia that I seek these deeper familial connections abroad. The best advice I ever received as a new traveller starting out was 'Find your mum wherever you go'. My parents are utterly irreplaceable, so it seemed like a ridiculous goal at first, but what this actually meant was: find the friends who you can love like family. Find the protectors who will look out for you and keep you safe; the guides who are happy to show you how to walk, talk, eat and live in this strange new world. And if you're lucky enough to find these rare human gems while wandering the Earth, respect and honour them as you would your own mother.

Looking around the table now I see five people from four countries who I have chosen to be my family.

Gratefully, I realise they've all chosen me back.

Not because I cook rice and produce lots of children. Not because I have only one glass of wine with dinner. Not because I fit into their lives, adapt to their cultures or speak their languages like they do. They love me despite the fact I don't do *any* of those things. Just as I love them. Every day, Aama sees me failing at the only measure of womanhood she's ever known, yet she respects and trusts me enough to welcome me into her home and family. To fly her halfway around the world and keep her safe, fed and cared for in a foreign land. Our entire relationship has been built on the foundation of difference, so maybe she's not judging me at all.

Maybe I'm judging myself.

And then it dawns on me.

The wine.

Maybe this isn't even about me.

Maybe she's not telling me *I'm* not allowed to have another glass. What if this is Aama's roundabout way of asking if *she* can have another one for herself? Drinking wine is frowned upon for women in Nepali culture and greed is equally shameful, so Aama will only serve herself if there is some left over after everyone else is satisfied. So, if I say I'm satisfied, there's no need for more wine.

'Yes,' I smile up at Eefke. 'Please. I'd love another glass of wine.'

Eefke reaches for the bottle opener, pulls the cork out with a satisfying pop and hands the bottle to me across the table.

'Would you like a glass of wine, Aama?' I tilt the neck of the bottle towards her. She gives a coy smile and casts a glance towards Baba to check his reaction. When there's none, she looks back to the bottle of wine.

'Maybe just a little one,' Aama holds up her thumb and finger a few centimetres apart, and the wine makes a delicious glug glug glug noise as I fill her glass to the brim.

72

Aama has no idea it's her birthday until she emerges bleary-eyed from her bedroom and we all start singing 'Happy Birthday' at her in three languages when she sits down for breakfast.

'Today is *my* birthday?' Aama's hand flies to her chest.

'Yes, it is,' I step forward holding a box wrapped in coloured paper, tied with ribbon.

'Well, what day is it then?' Aama chortles and we all start laughing.

'It's the sixth of September in our calendar, and the twentieth of Bhadra in yours.'

'So how old am I?'

'You're sixty-four!'

'Sixty-four years old and this is my first ever birthday,' Aama beams, her eyes creasing with delight as we place the colourful boxes in front of her. 'What do I do with these?'

'They're presents. You take the paper off to find your gifts inside,' David explains.

Aama coos, ripping off the wrapping to reveal a soft handmade pashmina and a shiny, silver Italian coffee pot.

We're spending the weekend at Jen's parents' house in the western town of Deventer. Stepping inside Bas and Mieke's home has been like being pulled in for a bear hug. Ever since we've arrived they've been showering endless love on us in the form of pancakes and pastries, and their endless positivity is infectious. On our last full day together, we wander through the local streets and outdoor markets in town. As the day heats up, Bas directs us into a dessert shop that is 'world famous in Deventer', and Aama insists on buying everyone a tiny pot of ice cream to celebrate her birthday. We argue that it's tradition that the birthday girl should never pay, but Aama holds out a firm hand to silence us.

'This is not a discussion. I can never repay you for what

you've done for Baba and me on this trip, but I *can* buy you an ice cream on my birthday.' Then she hands over the equivalent of three weeks of her daughter's full-time teaching salary so we can spend ten minutes eating chocolate, pistachio and *stroopwafel* ice cream from little cardboard pots. It is pure indulgence and, for better or worse, it appears something of Europe's hedonism may have rubbed off on Aama.

73

It's our last night in Bas and Mieke's home and we're gathered around their candlelit wooden dining table, sipping syrupy red wine from crystal glasses. The Dutch have a word to describe the warm, fuzzy feeling that lights your soul in moments like these, but it doesn't translate well into English. Similar to the Scandinavian *hygge*, Dutch *gezelligheid* can be a connection with wonderful friends, or new ones; when you laugh from your belly, exchange stories, eat well and share a cosy, heartwarming moment together. Often by candlelight. It's a hybrid emotion or state of being I've heard aptly described as an 'inner summer'.

Across the table, Jen rises from her chair and signals for Leon to join her. They make their way to the centre of the living room and pick up their violins.

Aama has been waiting years for this moment.

Jen has spoken with Aama often about the instrument she

plays as part of an orchestra that tours the world, but she could never bring her beloved violin to the village. Aama can only imagine it sounds something like the Nepali *serengi,* a string instrument that makes a metallic screeching noise that always sounds to me like a train braking.

Jen and Leon press their chins to their violins and, with the gentle downward stroke of horsehair against strings, a deep elegant tone fills the room. The slow, haunting melody holds us all in a trance, the music so rich and full it seems to occupy all the empty space around us. I look around the table and see Bas and Mieke overflowing with pride. Aama's cheeks are wet and Baba's eyes are brimming with tears. David has his eyes closed. No one moves.

'That song was for you, Aama, for your birthday,' Jen says in a soft voice after the final tone evaporates from the air and she brings her violin down. 'When you think of me, maybe the melody will come to you.'

Wiping her scarf against the tears falling down her face, Aama smiles up at her Dutch daughter. 'Do you remember, Sonni? Do you remember when you were in Sundara you tried to explain to me what the violin is and what it sounds like? But I couldn't imagine it. You talked to me about your parents and told me how one day you hoped we would all meet, and you could show me how to play the violin? Well today, finally, that day has come.'

Aama turns to David and me, her voice cracking.

'All of my biggest dreams have come true!' Fresh tears tumble down Aama's cheeks and she presses two hands against her heaving chest. 'And all the dreams I didn't know I could dream, they came true as well. Because of you my Laura Maya *buhari*, David *chora*. Because of you, I have nothing left to dream.'

I bow my head as deep as it will go and I sniff back the tears, setting off a Mexican wave of emotional snuffles around the table. No one speaks because nothing can be said. Our time together is coming to an end. Tomorrow we will return to France and in just a few days this wild adventure will all be over. When we set out on this journey, we had no idea what would happen. There were so many unknowns and it often felt like an impossible dream that we could never pull off. But we did it. We've opened windows on each other's worlds that used to be walls, and our lives will never be the same again.

The metallic groan of the bow grazing the steel violin strings brings us all back into the room. A mischievous grin spreads across Jen's face and she does a little upper body jig before launching into a spirited Irish song. Her violin is now a fiddle, and she taps the rhythm against the floor as she plays, calling us all to our feet. Soon, we're all stomping and clapping along, cheering Jen on as she picks up speed. Then she throws herself onto the floor on her back, kicking her feet in the air, but still never misses a beat. In tears just moments before, now everyone in the room is roaring with laughter as she plays faster and faster and faster until she collapses, her limbs flopping out to the sides like a starfish.

The room erupts, all of us stamping and applauding as Jen stands up and bows to her small, adoring crowd. I touch both hands to my flushed cheeks and shake my head when I realise they're wet again. This time with tears of laughter.

Far out, I can't keep up …

74

We sing 'Happy Birthday' again when Aama's cake is brought out for dessert with more than twenty candles blazing. Aama and Baba both sit back in their chairs, distancing themselves from the flames placed in front of her.

'Aama, it's tradition in our culture that when you look at the candles, you make a wish,' I explain. 'You think of your biggest dream then you blow the flames out so it can come true.'

'What dream?' Aama explodes. 'I just told you I have no dreams left. Look at me, I'm in Europe! I've flown in an aeroplane! I've seen the mountains of Switzerland and the moon pulling on the ocean! I've eaten delicious skinny potato things, watched rainbow rain fall in the night sky and had people treat me like the Queen of Nepal. Now, I'm celebrating my first ever birthday. What dreams could possibly be left?'

Aama looks back down at her cake and watches the candles for a moment, the amber light flickering on her face. Then she gives a determined nod and looks back up at the faces gathered around her. 'My dream is that all of *your* dreams come true.'

Aama takes in a deep breath, puffs her cheeks and attempts

to blow out the candles. She employs the same technique she uses to turn a dwindling pile of ash on her kitchen fire back into a blazing flame and unfortunately it has a similar effect on her birthday cake. She blows and blows, but the tiny flames barely quiver. She huffs and puffs, but not one candle is extinguished. Sitting next to her, Baba chuckles; quietly at first, his shoulders bobbing up and down. But as Aama starts to hyperventilate and her candles refuse to die, Baba is laughing so hard he's clutching his belly, doubled over, struggling to breathe.

'What are you *laughing* at?' Aama exhales, exasperated.

'They set your food on fire!' Baba roars.

Aama's frustration turns to an amused smile and she looks up at me with that trademark expression.

'Why *did* you light my cake on fire?'

'It's tradition,' I shrug. 'Just something we do on people's birthdays.'

'But *why*?' Aama insists, and I remember back to the unexplainable spoonful of milk Kashi poured down my throat when we left the village.

'I don't know, Aama,' I laugh and shrug again. 'We just do.'

75

Aama and Baba's journey ends as it began almost one month ago, only in reverse. Before we go back to Paris for their return flights to Nepal, we retreat to Véronique's home in her sleepy, seaside village in Normandy. It's a chance for all of us to exhale, prepare for their departure and reflect on everything we've been through. We spend long, lazy afternoons grazing around the outdoor dinner table and pottering in the garden. On the swinging lounge, Aama uses one foot to propel herself and Baba back and forth, in and out of the sunshine. A month ago they wanted to go back to Nepal because they had no work and no purpose, but now they're dozing in the afternoon sun, snoring softly. Blissfully doing nothing.

We take this time to put together a photo diary of our trip. We print about ninety photos and go through one by one so I can write a little note detailing what they remember about the moment it was taken. We want them to be able to share their experience with their friends and family in Nepal, but also for them to have these memories to look back on when, a few months from now, it will all feel like a dream.

As I'm organising the album, Aama picks up an image of the four of us in front of the historic village of Le Mont St Michel. She studies the photo, contemplating the huge monastery that stands behind us on an island reaching to the sky from the sea.

'When we spend all our lives in our own little world, the place where we have always lived, we only see what we know, don't we?' Aama muses. 'And we only know what we see. So how can we have new ideas and find better ways to do things if we always see things done the same way?'

She puts the photo down and picks up one of a group of people at the wedding.

'And if we don't make an effort to meet people who are different from us, we'll never find out just how much we're all the same.' She puts down the photo and looks up at me. 'I understand you now. I understand why you travel so much. It's good to leave our little world sometimes so we can go experience other people's worlds. Because when we learn how others live, we also learn about ourselves. That makes us better people, don't you think? After just one month, I won't go back to Nepal as the same woman who left.'

On her first ever holiday, Aama has reached the same conclusion as one of the greatest explorers and travel writers of all time, who said:

> Travel is fatal to prejudice, bigotry, and narrow-mindedness, and many of our people need it solely on these accounts. Broad, wholesome, charitable views of men and things cannot be acquired by vegetating in one little corner of the earth all one's lifetime.

After four weeks in Europe, Aama is basically Mark Twain.

Many well-travelled people will never reach this realisation. These days, you can visit a hundred countries and see thousands of tourist sights without interacting with the local culture. Even when we plan an adventure with cultural exploration in mind, it's unusual that we can surrender to a journey like Aama and Baba have on this trip. We're usually in control of our own travels and we have a bottomless internet pit of information to draw on, so we can book our accommodation, plan our excursions and make dinner reservations before we've even left home. We can follow the local hashtags on social media and check out the 'must sees' on travel review sites, so we have our entire journey mapped out and a heart full of expectations before we board the plane.

We have a friend in Nepal, a Canadian ex-bikie gang member, who often laments this aspect of modern society. He's in his seventies and always wears a baseball cap pulled so low that between the visor and his long grey beard we can barely see his eyes and nose. You'll find him in the streets fixing the local families' bicycles, with a tool in one hand and a can of Heineken in the other, always having a rant about something.

One thing he said has always stayed with me, but to get the full impact you have to read it in the North American drawl of a pissed-off old bikie. He said:

> Back in the classical era, we had *wisdom*. Philosophers sitting around on rocks asking the big questions. Back then, people looked inward to try and understand humans, the world and how we're all connected. Then came the so-called Age of Enlightenment, which was all about *knowledge*. Scientists conducting experiments, trying to understand how to harness nature and develop technology. Now our technology has surpassed us. We're living in the Information Age and that's all we've got: *shit tonnes of information*. A bunch

of idiots sitting behind their computers barking instructions, telling other people how to live. Now when we want to know something we don't ask ourselves questions. We don't look inside. We don't experiment. We just go online and Google shit until we're convinced we're going to die.

I've thought about this a lot while we've been travelling with Aama and Baba; how rare it is to embark on a journey completely unencumbered by information or expectations. They approached this adventure as an experiment, and they only had their wisdom to draw on. When they encountered something new or strange, they often responded with introspection instead of outward judgement. This is travel mastery. This trip has been an exercise in learning to appreciate things for what they are, not what they are in comparison to something or somewhere else. Through Aama and Baba's eyes, I have been able to see old things in new ways and perform my most mundane daily rituals as if they were all happening for the first time. What a heart-bursting gift it's been to see the things I consider boring and normal now sparkling with so much wonder. I've always been an advocate for slow travel, but this trip has taught me I can still take it further, to be more curious about life's little details. Like the texture and shape of the leaves that grow on the vines of the grapes of the wine I drink with my dinner ... the temperature of the supermarket floor ... what happens to the corn in the fields next to the autoroute I travel along every day ... and whether the people I love are lonely or alone. If nothing else, this trip has taught me to ask better questions about the things around me that I realise now I've never bothered to question at all.

76

We return to Paris at night so Aama and Baba can see why it's called the City of Lights. We take the glass elevator up the Eiffel Tower to look down on the city from a great, giddy height, and Aama almost loses her lunch. It's *chakai pariyo*, of course, but she's too terrified to enjoy it, insisting the tower is infinitely more beautiful when observed with both her feet planted safely on earth.

As Aama and I wander, arms linked, beneath the giant metal feet of the Eiffel Tower on our way back to the car, I remember what she said before she blew out her birthday candles.

'You know, Aama, when I was a little girl *this* was my big dream,' I point up at the looming metal pyramid. 'I saw pictures of the Eiffel Tower on TV and in books and I hoped and dreamed that one day I would visit Paris. Then, many years later, I met David and I fell in love with him before I even knew where he was from. The first time I ever came to Paris was to see him. He brought me straight to the Eiffel Tower, then he kissed me right at the moment it started sparkling like a million fireflies. It was just like a Bollywood movie. That day, my biggest dream came true, just like your dream has come true now.'

Aama smiles and looks from me to the tower rising above us. 'So what did you do after all your dreams came true?'

'After a while, I made some new dreams. And those dreams led us to you in Nepal. So, I know you feel like all your dreams have come true now, but after everything you've seen and done on this trip, maybe some new ideas will come to you?'

'That's true. I've been thinking I could build another room and grow my homestay business?' Aama looks to me for approval and I nod to encourage her. 'Then if I have a little more money from that, I could take another holiday. Somewhere in Nepal. I could even go to Lumbini and see where Buddha was born.'

Aama's eyes sparkle as the idea forms, the seeds of a new dream planted under the gigantic, glittery radio antenna where so many other people's dreams come true.

77

Our close family friend, Fabrice, joined us for our trip up the Eiffel Tower and now we're driving him home to his apartment in Paris. After he wishes Aama and Baba a heartfelt farewell, we watch him walk to the front door and wait until he's safely inside before driving home.

'Is his family in there waiting for him?' Aama whispers beside me.

'No, he lives alone.'

Aama shoots me a confused look, 'How old is he?'

'Thirty-eight, I think.'

'And he doesn't have a wife?' Aama asks, and I shake my head. 'Why not? Doesn't he want to get married and have children?'

'Yeah, he does want marriage and children, I think.'

'What's the problem then?'

'He just hasn't found someone to love yet.'

'Well, of course he hasn't found love, he's not married yet,' Aama throws her hands up in the air as Fabrice disappears behind his front door. 'Why don't his parents step in and find someone for him?'

'That's not how it works here, remember? We have to find our own husband or wife. First we find love, then we get married.'

'So how do you find love?'

I squirm and adjust my seatbelt, stalling while I think of an honest response. How *do* you find love in our culture?

'Well, we seek out ways to meet different people, so we might go to a bar or out to a party. We might find someone we like at work or school. If not, we can go onto our phones and use a special network to find other single people who are also looking for love. Or we can take up a hobby or sport, like joining a jogging club, to find people who like the same things as us.'

Aama's face lights up. 'Aha, so that's why you people run around getting all sweaty!' Finally, this mysterious 'sport' thing has a purpose. 'Where did you meet David?'

'In a hotel bar in Peru.'

'And Alain and Elena?'

'He was her mother's taxi driver in Paris.'

'And Damian and Lea?'

'They met at work in Ireland, in an office.'

'Ehh, okay, so you meet and then what happens?'

'Well, first you start talking on the phone or email, or you meet for coffee or dinner. You spend time together. Then if you like each other, you might stay together for a while so it's like you're married, but you're not. That way you can see if you're a good match.'

'Ugh, that sounds exhausting,' Aama scrunches her face. 'For us, it's easy. Our parents know us well and they choose us a good match right from the beginning. Then we get married and we fall in love. Not right away, but eventually. What happens if you realise you're not a good match?'

'Then you break up and start the whole process from the beginning, looking for someone else. If you want to.'

'But humans aren't perfect!' Aama throws her hands up again. 'Everyone has something wrong with them and there are always problems, even when both people try really hard. If you don't get married right away, what stops people from just giving up when things get difficult?'

Oof. Great question ...

'Nothing, I guess. It only works if both people are compatible and really want it to work.'

I kind of see where Aama is coming from because my experience with David was closer to an arranged marriage than the normal trajectory of a relationship in my culture. We'd hooked up a few times over the years, but technically we were only dating for nine weeks before we got married, and we didn't move in with each other until six weeks after the wedding. That's when we realised we were *completely* different people with polar opposite ideas about how to run a household.

When we announced our surprise engagement, my mum told us that to make a marriage work we needed to agree on the three big things: Where do we want to live? How many children do we want? And how should we manage our money? Everything else, she said, could probably be worked out along the way. This was comforting not only because we *did* agree on the big things, but because we discovered we couldn't agree on *any* of the little things. Sometimes the only thing that stopped us giving up on each other was knowing we'd stood up in front of 200 friends and family and promised we wouldn't. Since then, I've fallen in love with my husband thousands of times in countless different ways. And it's not the same kind of love that drew us together in the first place.

Aama is right about at least one thing: all the people in my life who are single and actively seeking a life partner are exhausted by the process. They're tired of dating and 'selling' themselves, or having their hopes crushed when another promising new relationship fails in the first few weeks. They're sick of spending money on coffees and movie tickets and fancy dinners shared with people they never want to see again. Not to mention my female friends who are shelling out thousands of dollars to have their eggs frozen because they're in their thirties and Mr Right is still Mr Where the Hell Is He? Then, when you do find someone you like, that's only half the battle won. Next, you have to work out how to seem keen so they stay interested, but not too desperate that you scare them away. It's a game millions of people are playing, but no one knows the rules. Yet still, somehow, most of us would choose all that drama and uncertainty over letting our parents set us up.

'What happens if Fabrice never finds someone to love? How can he have the children he wants?'

'Well, he can't, really,' I grimace. 'A woman can have a baby without a man, but it's harder for a man to have children without a woman.'

The truth feels uncomfortable laid out like this.

'Well, I think that all sounds too hard,' Aama gives a disapproving cluck. 'All that searching and searching and you might never find what you're looking for! You know what we'll do? You send Fabrice to me in Nepal. He seems like a lovely man. He's handsome and he's got a good job and a house. He's an easy sell! I could find him ten wives tomorrow and I swear on my buffalo, he'll be in love by the end of the year.'

78

'*Sunnuchha* Baba?'

Baba's head jerks up to look at David, who is standing on the opposite side of the room.

'*Ho*,' Baba confirms with a single nod, 'I can hear you.'

Aama gasps. Then she turns and walks away from Baba and mutters some words into her armpit in Gurung.

Baba immediately turns his head to look at his wife.

'I can hear you,' he says.

The room erupts in excited cheers and applause. After more than thirty years living in silence, the grin on Baba's face stretches from new hearing aid to new hearing aid.

Earlier in our trip, a family friend found out Baba was deaf and offered up his mother's old hearing aids. 'They're worth three thousand euros,' he said, 'but she refuses to wear them because she says they make her feel like Robocop.'

It takes some fussing around with batteries and remote controls, but now they're installed and Baba can *hear*. He spends the day spinning around, his head following the faint meow of a cat, the rumbling engine of a plane flying overhead and the soft music playing in a shopping centre elevator.

But the real game changer is how clearly Baba *speaks* now that he can hear the sound of his own voice. Instead of zoning out when we're all gathered around the table for our last meal, Baba is now alert and involved. He nods along with the conversation and even interjects to offer his own point of view.

'How do I leave?' Aama asks, sliding one finger around the rim of her empty water glass, lost in thought. 'We spend all these weeks together, exploring new places and living a whole new life. Now it's like the other life doesn't even exist. So how do we leave here and say goodbye?' Her voice cracks.

'It's difficult,' Baba agrees, crooning in his smooth, new voice. 'It was hard leaving Nepal because we didn't know where we were going, but we always knew we would come home. When we leave here, it's harder. We know we will probably never come back, but there are people we care about in both places so it's like being split in two.'

We all nod. *Yep, you hit it right on the nose my wise, poetic, all-knowing, all-hearing Baba.*

If Aama is Mark Twain, then Baba is anthropologist Miriam Adney, who famously said:

> You will never be completely at home again
> because part of your heart will always be elsewhere.
> That's the price you pay for the richness of loving
> and knowing people in more than one place.

With a break in the conversation, Baba chooses this moment to rise from his seat. He stands with his hands on the table and looks around at us all with a mischievous grin. We look up at him, thinking he's about to make a speech, but instead he reaches out and grabs a serving spoon. Then he drives it into the bowl of rice in the centre of the table. In an awkward gesture, he moves a mound of fluffy white grain to his plate then goes back for the vegetables. Slippery strips of capsicum slip off the spoon and onto the tablecloth, but he picks them up with his fingers and piles them on top of his rice with a splatter. As he does this, everyone at the table puts their cutlery down and watches on in shock.

Baba sits down and looks at both sides of the table with a gummy smile. 'What? You said the men of this country have to serve themselves if they're hungry. Well, I need to store some energy, I'm flying halfway around the world tonight!'

Everyone goes *nuts*. We all drumroll on the table, whoop and stamp our feet as Baba takes a mouthful of the first food I've ever seen him eat that wasn't served to him by a woman.

79

Baba's transformation that day whips up a storm of emotions in my chest I don't know what to do with. While the conversation turns to Aama and Baba's heaving suitcases (our ultra-minimalists are going home with three), I excuse myself to the bathroom where I sit on the toilet and ugly cry into half a roll of pink toilet paper.

I'm happy for Baba—thrilled that he's back in the world, hearing again and serving himself food when he's hungry—but these aren't just happy tears. They're everything tears. They're tears of sadness that we all have to say goodbye today. Tears of joy that Aama and Baba were brave enough to stay the full month and that we've all become so close. Tears of regret that I didn't realise restoring Baba's hearing would also bring his soul to life. And tears of frustration that we didn't get these bloody hearing aids at the *beginning* of this trip—a suggestion we had made back in Nepal that Baba had immediately rejected. These last few weeks were the best opportunity we would ever have to get to know Baba, and now it's over.

I'd love to tell you we all put on our happy faces to give Aama and Baba a joyful send off, but we don't and the trip to the airport is a weeping funeral march. By the time we're all buckled into the car, every single one of us is in tears. Baba, David and Véronique are all blurry-eyed and sniffing back their emotions, but Aama and I are sitting in the back, clinging to each other, blubbering. I can't explain why we're so inconsolable, it's not like we'll never see each other again. It feels like all the emotions we've felt since this journey was just an idea are now bubbling to the surface with nowhere to go but up and out.

'I'm so happy,' Aama weeps. 'I'm crying but I'm not in pain. When I think of everything we've seen and done together this month, I've honestly never been so happy in my life. Some people walk through the world with no family at all and I am lucky to have three, so we can't cry.' Aama trips on these final words and bursts into fresh tears, which sets everyone else off again.

'I said stop crying!' Aama wails, laughing and choking on her own sobs.

We're still half an hour from the airport when I remember a song I once heard sung in the village at the end of a big event.

Last year, we helped seventeen villagers become qualified bee breeders. The idea was the community would purchase commercial beehives and create a honey-bottling business on the mountain. To achieve this goal, they had to complete a five-day course that came with some huge personal obstacles. Many of them couldn't read or write, and they had to juggle their studies around their full load of house and farm work. Despite this, at the end of the week, every participant passed their diploma. At the graduation ceremony, they each rose to thunderous applause as their names were called to shake the teacher's hand and receive their certificate. For some of them, this was the first time in their lives a personal achievement was recognised on paper.

After their graduation, the villagers sat in a circle and performed a joyful and heartfelt song to reflect on what they had accomplished. Each new verse started with *'Ke gardyo, ke gardyo, ke gardyo, ke gardyo'*, which asks four times, 'What did we do?'. Then they each took turns improvising the next lyrics, singing about the things they experienced during their training. They sang about sticking their hands into beehives and getting stung ten times, and they sung about pulling beehives apart and racing each other to see who could put them back together the fastest. The crowd laughed as they sang and the women spun around the courtyard, dancing to the beat of the drum with pride as the community reflected on all the things they accomplished together.

So, as we hurtle towards the airport, I launch into the same song: '*ke gardyo, ke gardyo, ke gardyo, ke gardyo* … we saw so much corn, such fat cows and a tiny car that lets you cut grass sitting down …'

Everyone cracks up and David leaps in with the next verse: '*ke gardyo, ke gardyo, ke gardyo, ke gardyo* … we ate so much cheese, cold cheese, hot cheese and cheese that stinks like feet …'

Now Aama joins in: '*ke gardyo, ke gardyo, ke gardyo, ke gardyo* … we became the King and Queen of Nepal and Baba danced like a galloping horse.'

And so it goes on, all of us taking turns to throw in a verse. Aama and I hold tight to each other's hands and sing our hearts out as we hurtle towards the airport. We sing until the tiny aeroplane symbols became more prominent on the road signs above, and the bellies of low-flying jumbos appear overhead. Then as we swing around the looping road into the underground car park and stop at the ticket barrier, Baba turns his head towards the centre of the car and blinks dramatically.

'We're here.'

80

The last time we see Aama and Baba in France they're both seated in wheelchairs, looking terrified and distraught in the clutches of two burly airport attendants. Of the two of them,

Baba seems the more anxious about the journey ahead, worried about how they'll manage without us.

'We've arranged wheelchair support for you all the way to Kathmandu so as long as you sit here and don't move, there will *always* be someone looking out for you,' David reassures him.

I've made them both an A4 flyer that states their full name, nationality, languages, passport number, flight numbers and a message to call us on the phone number provided in case of any problem. I also drew a glass of water, a bottle of beer and a goblet of wine, so if they're feeling thirsty or nervous they can ask a flight attendant for a liquid solution.

They're ready. Physically, we've prepared them for just about any event.

'Alright, we're off,' one of the gruff airport attendants barks, grabbing hold of the handles on Baba's wheelchair.

We've been dreading this moment all day but now there's nothing more that can be said. We hug them each in turn, Baba leaning in for the first and maybe last real hug I'll ever get without him giving himself whiplash.

When I turn to Aama, she cups my cheeks in her hands. 'Thank you for showing me your world, Laura Maya.'

'Thank you for showing me my own world through your eyes, Aama,' I pull her in for one last hug and she sobs into my shoulder, her glass bangles clinking softly as she tightens her grip around my neck.

The elevator leading up to the departure gates is only big enough to fit one person, so they have to go one by one. We hold Aama's hand as Baba goes first, wheeled into the elevator backwards so he can see us wave goodbye. Just before the doors close we start jumping up and down, blowing kisses and yelling that we love him. He cracks a gummy smile, chuckling at our embarrassing public display of affection, then the doors gobble him up and whisk him away.

As the airport attendant hits the elevator button and prepares Aama to wheel in backwards, I stand in front of her chair. Then, just as I've seen Kashi do countless times, I reach down to touch Aama's feet and bow my head. I've never done it before because I rejected the idea that a woman should bow at anyone's feet, but today it feels like an honour. I have no idea what it means or if I'm doing it right. I don't really care. I only hope she knows it's a symbol of the deep respect I hold for her and the relationship we share. Whatever labels it carries. Whether we understand each other or not.

Soon, her wheelchair is backed into the elevator and David, Véronique and I leap and yelp and laugh and dance until a tiny smile creases the corners of her glistening eyes.

'See you again, Aama!' we scream into the air, as the giant steel doors close around her and part of our hearts travels off to elsewhere.

PART 5

Back in Nepal

No matter where you're from, your dreams are valid.
—*Lupita Nyong'o*

81

'What do you mean the village closed down?' I press my hand against my heart to stop it leaping out. 'Where did everybody go?'

We're back in Nepal and I'm in the library with about fifteen students and Tara, the librarian, whose salary we're funding. Tara and I are sorting through a box of books that have been donated by a Singaporean NGO, including fourteen mouldy copies of *Twilight*, three incomplete versions of *Gone with the Wind* and a series of French books about the global economy. All are completely useless and inappropriate for children who only speak Nepali (or children who speak any language, for that matter) and we're putting them aside for firewood.

I notice a girl I've never seen before, drawing and colouring with a group of kids from Tara's village. When I ask Tara, she tells me her name is Heena.

'She's living in our village now since hers closed down. You know the village that used to be further up the hill?'

Tara explains that the families all left, one by one. It was one of the poorest villages on the mountain, home to many Dalit families who have now moved overseas or to the city in search of work. It's too expensive to live and study in town, so some parents have left their children here with other families so they could continue their schooling on the mountain.

'What about Anisha?' I ask Tara. 'She was from that village.

Who's she living with now?'

Tara scrunches up her nose and looks down at her hands.

'Tara?'

A wave of panic rushes into my throat.

'She was married,' Tara whispers.

'What?' I sit back on my heels and place a hand on the bookshelf to steady myself. 'She was only thirteen.'

'You know this sometimes happens in Nepal,' Tara says with a sad smile. 'Anisha's father left the family. Her mother wanted to marry another man, but he didn't want her children, so they arranged Anisha's marriage.'

'To who? Where?'

'I don't know who he is,' Tara shakes her head. 'All I know is she's gone to live on another mountain now with her husband's family. I'm sorry.'

'Don't be sorry, it's not your fault,' I brush it off, realising I've put her in an awkward position. 'Thank you for letting me know.'

We both go back to sorting our books into piles and I pick up a rat-eaten copy of *Twilight*. The image on the front is two arms outstretched, holding an apple. My mind travels back in time to when Anisha stood before me with her frail arms outstretched, begging for food. A piece of fruit. A biscuit. Anything to quieten the storm in her ravenous belly. I think about her standing at the library window, watching the other students play, too angry to come inside. I remember the day she felt brave enough to step through the door. The first time she giggled while reading a book.

Then my mind takes me back to Kolkata, to the young girl rescued from sex slavery whose face looked so much like Anisha's it lit a raging fire in my soul. Anisha brought me back to Nepal, and the day we arrived she marched right up to me and asked me in English if I remembered her. If only she knew.

I flash back to all those moments since ... sitting on the carpet in the library while she painted my toenails and plaited my hair ... doing puzzles and drawing flowers ... reading comic books together and talking about our dreams.

Now I imagine her as a wife. Barely a teenager. Separated from her family. Removed from school. Probably pregnant. A daughter-in-law, carrying the heavy weight of responsibility that comes with that title. I bite down hard on my lip to fight back the tears trying to push their way to the surface. *How dare I sit here crying when I have access to the kind of freedom and opportunities Anisha could never imagine?*

Not for the first time, I wonder if all the work we've done in the village is pointless, or at least inadequate. So far, I can't see that we're changing much for these girls. What's the use of them reading *I Am Malala* if their own parents will never fight for their education? Why waste time building towers out of Lego when their parents can't afford to repair the houses that are supposed to shelter them from the cold? How much can we really change with games, books and building blocks?

The sound of a screaming child snaps me out of my daze, and I look up to see a group of kids wrestling with a broken cardboard box. It looks like they're fighting and I move to intervene, but then the contents of the box explodes and they all start laughing. With excited squeals, one child grabs a square cardboard spinner, and two others unfold an enormous piece of white plastic. It has twenty-four perfect circles painted on it in red, yellow, blue and green.

Twister.

My eyes are still misty as I watch the kids throw themselves into the game. Each turn, someone flicks the spinner while the others twist themselves into increasingly awkward positions. Left foot yellow, right hand red, left hand blue, right foot green. Now four children are tangled together, limbs entwined, and their shrieking laughter is reverberating off the whitewashed concrete walls.

All four of these boys have been coming to the library since it first opened. While they play, I do a mental stocktake of their names and which village they're from, and a realisation dawns on me. This isn't just four ordinary kids playing Twister. This is four children from three different caste groups tangled together like a pretzel. The two boys in the middle are a Brahmin and a Gurung. The younger child struggling not to eat the plastic on the bottom and the older child trying not to collapse on top of everyone are both Dalits. Formerly untouchables. Six years ago, when we first met these children, they wouldn't have played together on the same team. Now they're making a human sandwich out of each other.

In this moment I feel a tiny glimmer of hope. The road to equality is not a French highway. It's a winding dirt track up a Himalayan mountain that sometimes washes away in the monsoon and has to be rebuilt. The girls we've come to love in the village probably can't change the destiny their parents have mapped out for them, but maybe ... hopefully ... they'll be able to choose a different path for their own children.

82

That afternoon, I drag my feet through the village on my way home from school, past the tiny Buddhist temple and along the stone pathways back to the house. I lock myself in the tiny concrete shower stall the family has built for us and crouch naked on the concrete floor, scooping buckets of ice-cold water over my head. The freezing water hits me like an electric shock and knocks the air from my lungs. Stunning me. Cleansing me. Waking me up.

Back in my room, I whip my dripping hair into a towel turban and reach for my *lungi*. I wrap it around my waist, threading its sash through a hole, and I pull it tight around my hips. Then I stop and take a deep sigh. *You don't need to do this anymore, Laura.*

I pull off the *lungi* in one swift movement and cast it aside on the bed. Then I retrieve a pair of baggy pants from my backpack and put those on instead. Straight away I feel more like myself. I pick up the *lungi*, fold it into a square and place it on the windowsill. It's time to pass it on to a woman in the village who will wear it better than me. The people of this community don't expect me to change who I am or dress like them any more than I expected Aama and Baba to put on a pair of jeans in France and eat a holy beef steak. They were brave and open to every experience—even willing to suspend entire belief systems and explore dizzying new ways of seeing the world—but they remained true to themselves throughout. They adapted to our culture respectfully without feeling the need to adopt it, and now I need to do the same here.

I've realised it *is* possible for Nepal and I to be deeply, madly in love with each other, without either one of us forcing the other to change. I've spent years trying to live up to my role as daughter-in-law of the village chief so I would belong in this village, with these people who stole my heart. I guess I felt like I could never help them or make a difference until I proved I could be one of them, but now I know I'll never be an integral part of this community. There's a limit to how much I'll ever be able to help. And that's okay. We probably helped the community more by giving their most prominent change-maker a front row seat to the world than we ever could with all our other projects combined. Now I understand that although I may never fit in here, I *do* belong. Just not in the way I thought I should.

83

Aama and her neighbour are sitting on a woven mat preparing dinner and I drop down to sit cross-legged beside them, picking up a handful of beans. The neighbour has just returned from visiting her family so it's the first time I've seen her since last year.

'You're back, Laura Maya!' she cries with delight. 'No baby yet?'

I open my mouth to respond but Aama waves a bangled hand in the air in front of my face, so I close it again.

'Laura Maya doesn't need a baby!' Aama dismisses her neighbour. 'She's got our Sristi and a hundred kids at the school to buy books for, what does she need her own baby for? Right, *buhari?*'

I blink at Aama, stunned. It's probably the same facial expression she gave me when I told her there were people floating in the air in a basket suspended from a giant balloon driven by a blazing fire.

'Yes. Right,' is all I manage. I'm too shocked to speak, but I feel my whole face stretching into a smile. I go back to peeling the beans, but there's a giggle rising in my chest that finds its way, breathlessly, out of my nose. Aama looks up at me with a satisfied grin and our eyes lock for a few precious moments, expressing all the feelings our words cannot. Gratitude, mostly. Acceptance. Belonging.

'Here, give me some of those beans,' Aama breaks our gaze and swoops her hand over my pile, taking back two-thirds of my beans to her side of the mat.

'I don't mind!' I protest at first. 'Although cooking is still not really my thing, is it?'

'Yeah, but it doesn't matter.' Aama waves a hand in the air again. 'You don't need to know how to shell beans or cook rice. Where you're from, you just press a few buttons and the machines will feed you. Or you can go down to the shop and buy some skinny delicious potato things. You're not going to starve!'

It's official. I can now hang up my *lungi* and end my impossible quest to become the perfect Nepali woman.

84

When we return to the village, we're surprised to find Baba no longer sits alone at his table in the kitchen, drinking *raksi* and rambling to himself. Instead, he sits with us around the fire and joins in the conversation. We talk a lot about our trip together, the memories they cherish and how their lives have changed since they came back.

'Do you remember the bridge?' Baba's eyes are wide as he raises his arms in front of him, re-enacting the moment the bridge disconnected from the street and reached up to the sky to let the boats pass. 'Sometimes I lie awake at night just trying to work out how they made that.'

'And that big tower,' Aama breathes out and smiles, now looking up to recall images of Paris in the same patch of air where she once tried to imagine them. 'To think your people had the technology to build that more than a hundred years ago and we're still cutting our grass by hand.'

'Those memories feel like dreams now,' Baba says, shaking his head.

'What has life been like since you came back to Nepal?' I ask. 'Was it difficult going back to work in the fields and taking care of the house after eating, sleeping and looking at stuff for a month?'

'Ah, we were fine. Why would it be difficult?' Aama pulls the pressure cooker full of *dhal* off the fire. 'We've lived more than sixty years like this and just one month in Europe. This is the life we know; we were happy to come back to it.'

'But I would have been happy to stay in Europe for a while longer too,' says Baba. 'Maybe three months.'

'What are you talking about?' Aama scoffs, pretending to throw a handful of rice in Baba's face so he flinches away from her. 'You wanted to leave after three days and come home, remember?'

'That's true!' Baba cackles and we all laugh.

'You know, in Europe we were the King and Queen of Nepal but when we came back, we became famous here, too,' Aama says. 'We're the first people on our mountain to travel the world like explorers. A lot of people go overseas for work, but not to visit so many places, have a holiday and experience all these new things. Now our name is known on this mountain. We hold the record. We are the first!' Aama holds up a triumphant finger.

'Everyone asks us, "But how is it possible you went to Europe? What was it like?"' Baba says, leaning towards David and me. 'And I always tell them Europe was heaven. Our son and daughter-in-law took us to heaven. And all I could give them in return was my thanks.'

'You give us a lot more than that, Baba,' I argue, giving him a playful nudge. 'You gave us a family and a home in Nepal. Without you, we would have been sleeping outside in the rice fields while we worked at the school all these years!'

'You could have slept with the buffalo,' Baba jokes, and Aama throws another playful handful of imaginary rice at him. 'I wouldn't want you to get eaten by a tiger.'

'So, has anything changed for you? Has life been different since coming home?'

Baba places his fist in front of his mouth and stares at the fire, gathering his thoughts. 'I understand the foreign people now. They come here and stay in our home, but I didn't know how to speak to them before because I didn't understand their ways. Now I know where they come from because I've seen it myself. And if I don't understand their behaviour, now I know it's probably because life is very different where they're from. Different in a way I can't imagine. So I just accept them for whoever they are.'

'And Baba doesn't talk so much at night,' Aama chimes in,

spooning rice onto five copper plates fanned out in front of her on the floor. 'That's changed. He doesn't sit at the table alone drinking *raksi* and talking to himself. He just sits here quietly now. I don't know why.'

'Why is that Baba?' I ask. 'Are you not happy?'

'I just have a lot to think about now,' Baba shrugs. 'You gave me a gift. Now I have thousands of beautiful moments I can daydream about for the rest of my life. When I'm quiet, it's because I'm watching them like a movie in my head.' Baba grins and twirls his finger in front of his face like a spinning film projector.

'What about you Aama?'

Aama pours *dhal* onto each of our plates and hands them to us. As I dig my fingers into the rice, she tucks her legs beneath her and adjusts her *lungi*, searching the air for an answer. 'I had some ideas for the house. New ways to decorate and things that can make our European guests more comfortable, like hot water they can use to wash. But the biggest changes are inside me. Life here in Nepal is the same, the house is the same, the village is the same, I'm the same on the outside, but inside I feel different. My mind is different.

'Sometimes I think back and remember I was so scared to leave Nepal that I almost didn't go. But then I saw that book, remember? With the old Gurung woman who went to America? And I thought if she can do it, I can do it. And off we went. Some of it was scary. The elevators, the moving stairs, the aeroplane and driving so fast in a car in the dark, *ah-ma-ma-ma-ma* I was terrified. But I did it all anyway.'

'Yes, you did,' I grin, 'and if I write a book about our adventure someday, someone might pick it up and see *your* picture inside. And maybe it will give them the courage to chase after *their* dreams that seem scary and impossible, too.'

'Ehhh,' Aama's eyes brighten at the thought. 'Maybe, eh? So you should write this book, Laura Maya *buhari*. Write about the good things your family has done in our village, and the way our two families came together as one. I can never pay you back for what you've done because I am not a rich woman. I have nothing to offer the world but my name. So take that and use it to show other people what is possible. Tell them my name and maybe it will help them believe their dreams can come true, too. Yes!

'Write this book, Laura Maya!

'Go tell the world that Dar Kumari Gurung went to Europe.'

Epilogue

Everything will be alright in the end.
So if it is not alright, then it is not yet the end.
—*Sonny Kapoor, The Best Exotic Marigold Hotel*

In March 2020, we were living back in Australia when David's phone lit up with an incoming call on Facebook Messenger. It was Kashi. Video calling. From Sundara. We couldn't believe it.

David hit the green button and suddenly he held our entire Nepali family in the palm of his hand. Baba waved at us and chuckled and Aama's grin stretched the entire width of David's iPhone as she moved in for an extreme close-up, pressing her nose to the screen and her palms together to greet us. She laughed and squealed with delight at the sight of our faces in Kashi's phone, but her tone quickly became serious.

'You two stay where you are!' She wagged a finger at us. 'You sit at home, you don't go out, you eat, you sleep and stay away from big groups of people. Do you hear me? You need to stay safe. There's a dangerous virus going around.'

Ten years earlier, there was no road, electricity, internet or even a newspaper in the village, but now Aama was video calling us on a smartphone to make sure we were social distancing and following proper coronavirus protocol. Life had certainly changed …

After their trip to Europe, Aama and Baba settled back into life in Nepal and the family built up their homestay business. Over the following years, they added two more bedrooms and welcomed over 500 guests from around the world into their home. They became Superhosts on Airbnb with 180 positive reviews. Travellers were excited to experience real Himalayan village life and find an 'Aama' to take care of them. With the homestay's income, more money could circulate within the mountain's micro-economy and create opportunities for other families. Aama and Baba also kept their job as part-time explorers. They've taken a couple of holidays in Nepal since returning home, leaving the village to go eat, sleep and look at stuff in their own country.

It didn't take long for Aama to make her new dreams come true. But the tree people have rotated in and out of power since we visited Switzerland and she is still waiting for her train.

When the coronavirus pandemic hit and the world went to ground, life in the village changed again. The tourists all left the country and the family's homestay business was put on hold. Not only did they lose their income within the space of a couple of weeks, they were cut off from the nearest city and unable to obtain any supplies. Once again, they were reminded that business and money were fickle and their true wealth was in their small, family-owned fields, which provided the only food they could access during the lockdown. In an interesting twist, a lot of families who had left their ancestral villages in search of work and a better life in the cities now returned to Sundara. Many felt safer in the mountain's wide-open spaces than they did in the virus-riddled city. So they came back and reclaimed their homes and fields, planting new crops of rice and vegetables, putting down roots and repopulating these once dwindling villages.

Although the book ends here, our story as a family is

still being written. To catch up on our latest news, you can connect with us at www.tellthemmyname.com. Even though we don't currently live in Nepal, most of our Nepali family are technologically equipped and we're more connected now than ever. We have an online group chat where we share photos and videos of our lives with each other most days, just like any ordinary family. As Aama and Baba don't use social media themselves, we send them videos and call them on the phone. Our Nepali is getting worse, not better, but no one cares. We call, tell them we miss them and love them, then we say 'See you again soon!' and hang up—even though we have no idea if and when we'll see each other again. We no longer have the vocabulary to hold the conversations we had during our great adventure, or when we spent several months each year in the Himalayas. Sometimes when we call them we find ourselves getting confused and speaking to them in a mix of random words and languages, but everyone just laughs. It doesn't matter. Our relationship has always defied logic and language and built its foundations on what is unspoken: an inexplicable trust and a deep knowing that our differences may scream and wail and stamp their feet the loudest, but they will never dim the light inside us that makes us all the same.

Acknowledgements

This book was written and published on Aboriginal land. I would like to acknowledge the traditional custodians of country throughout Australia and recognise their continuing connection to land, waters and community. I pay my respect to Elders past, present and emerging and acknowledge that sovereignty was never ceded.

It's important to note this book would never have happened without David. To my incredibly patient and unconditionally loving Frenchman, thank you for never giving up on me or this book, even though I did a few times. Thank you for the unwavering support and encouragement (read: ass-kicking) and the endless cups of tea ... *Je t'aime mon amour.*

To Aama, Baba and all our Nepali family, *dherai, dherai dhanyabad.* Thank you for welcoming us into your home, your lives and your family. Thank you for being our teachers and trusting us enough to embark on this wild adventure into the unknown. Even the 70,000+ words in this book aren't enough to express how much you all mean to us.

A special mention goes to Bisha, who joined our publishing team as an editor and cultural consultant. You helped make this a much better book and gave me the courage to share it with the world. Also, thanks to Dakshy for answering so many random language and cultural questions over the years while I was writing.

To *'ma belle famille'*, my in-laws in France, thank you for your love, support and making me feel like I belong in your family and culture even though I don't fit in. *Merci infiniment* for going above and beyond to throw your support behind the community in Nepal and for being instrumental in making this trip happen.

A special shout out to my mother-in-law—your courage embarking on that first trip to Nepal will always inspire me and this journey literally would not have been possible without your spirit of generosity.

To my inspiring, irreplaceable mum and dad—I won the parent lottery. Thank you for being my cheerleaders and the kind of parents who legitimately just want me to do what makes me happy. Thank you for holding this book dream so close but so lightly. I couldn't have done this without you.

Thank you to my beautiful sister—who is hands down *the* best friend to call when I'm having a writing meltdown—and my brother-in-law, nieces and nephews for always encouraging me even though I'm the 'crazy aunt' who zips in and out and misses lots of milestones. Thanks also to my extended family of cousins, aunts and uncles for your support.

An enormous heartfelt thanks goes to my editor and publisher Natasha Gilmour who wanted to publish this book before she'd even read it. I came to you a little fragile after my first brush with the traditional publishing world and you took this book and me on a journey that proved there could be another way. Your nurturing approach coupled with incredible knowledge and expertise in the industry has been a hot chocolate on a snowy day.

Thank you to all my contributing editors, especially Dr Juliet Richters and Emily 'Jungle Eyes' Miller, who helped me knock this manuscript into shape and make it a much better book. To my cover designer Nada Backovic—thank you for all the soul you put into your work and for making this book look like it's wrapped in magic. Thanks also to Sian Yewdall and Natasha Solomun from The Rights Hive. And a big shout out to Sam Wren Quan Sing and the team at Frank & Co for the thorough and insightful Sensitivity Read. I'm so grateful you've helped me become a better author and ally.

A big thanks to Gareth from the writing academy for the brutally honest manuscript evaluation and for telling me to start writing the book from scratch when, 5 years in, I thought I was finished. That hurt to hear but I'm happy I took your advice!

Special shout outs to Miha and Nina for your art. Gwen, Lothar and your family for your hospitality. Yaro for keeping me fed throughout the writing years. Sarita, Sangya and Asim (rest in peace, *sathi*) for your friendship. Prem for the early morning Nepali classes. Helena for being my reader muse, and Laoise for being my modern slavery lighthouse.

I feel unbelievably grateful that I have so many friends, family members and colleagues I want to thank personally that it would be impossible to list you all by name. I know how lucky I am to have that problem. But you know who you are, my special people all over the world. Even though I couldn't engrave your name on these pages, I want you to know your friendship and encouragement mean everything to me.

Thank you to everyone who hosted us during the trip, invited us to your wedding or took part in this adventure, even if you didn't know it! This journey changed all our lives forever.

Lastly, thank YOU. Whoever you are. I'm grateful you took the time to read our story.

About the author

Laura Maya

Laura Maya is a writer, coach and culturally curious 'digital nomad' who has spent over 20 years wandering slowly through almost 60 countries. *Tell Them My Name* (2022, the kind press) is her first book, and she is co-author of *This I Know Is True* (2021, the kind press). Laura identifies as a 'multipotentialite'—a hyper curious person who feels called to explore endless different careers, countries, hobbies and interests. She runs a coaching business helping women navigate change and step into the life they want, even if it's a life other people may not understand. Laura prides herself on living simply, chasing 'impossible' dreams and creating a life that supports and enhances the freedom of others. She usually lives between Australia, France, Nepal and Tonga and tries to explore everywhere in between.

lauramaya.com @lauramayawrites

Be part of the family!

Although the book ends here, our story continues ...

To find out what happened next, see photos from the trip, learn more about the issues discussed in this book and stay connected with our quirky international family, scan the QR code below, or visit us at **tellthemmyname.com**

Lightning Source UK Ltd.
Milton Keynes UK
UKHW011823060622
404004UK00003B/979